Jesus' B......
Jesus Grows Up
Jesus Is With Us

hands-On BiBLE curriculum™

Pre-K & K, Winter
Teacher Guide

Group
Loveland, Colorado

www.HandsOnBible.com

Group's R.E.A.L. Guarantee® to you:

This Group resource incorporates our R.E.A.L. approach to ministry—one that encourages long-term retention and life transformation. It's ministry that's:

Relational
Because learner-to-learner interaction enhances learning and builds Christian friendships.

Experiential
Because what learners experience through discussion and action sticks with them up to 9 times longer than what they simply hear or read.

Applicable
Because the aim of Christian education is to equip learners to be both hearers and doers of God's Word.

Learner-based
Because learners understand and retain more when the learning process takes into consideration how they learn best.

Group

Hands-On Bible Curriculum™, Pre-K & K, Winter
Copyright © 1995 Group Publishing, Inc.

2003 edition

Visit our Web site: **www.grouppublishing.com**

Credits
Contributing Authors: Robin Christy, Melissa C. Downey, and Nanette Goings
Editor: Jody Brolsma
Senior Editor: Lois Keffer
Chief Creative Officer: Joani Schultz
Copy Editor: Pamela Shoup
Art Director: Helen H. Lannis
Cover Art Director/Designer: DeWain Stoll
Designers: Lisa Chandler and Jean Bruns
Print Production Artist: Randy Kady
Cover Production Artist: Kevin Mullins
Cover Photographer: Daniel Treat
Illustrators: Judy Love, Bonnie Matthews, and Jim Connolly
Audio Producer: Steve Saavedra
Production Manager: Dodie Tipton

ISBN 0-7644-0369-9
Printed in the United States of America.
10 9 8 7 6 5   05 04 03

Contents

Which Age Level of Group's® Toddlers Through 6-Year-Olds Hands-On Bible Curriculum™ Is Right for Your Class?

Maximize your teaching success by choosing the curriculum that's best suited to the needs of the children you teach. With preschoolers, a few months can make a big difference in what works in the classroom and what doesn't! This overview shows how Group's® **Hands-On Bible Curriculum™ for Toddlers Through 6-Year-Olds** carefully tracks with developmental guidelines.

Toddlers & 2s

- colorful, three-dimensional Interactive StoryBoards™ with sensory items for children to touch, taste, and smell
- supervised play centers
- emphasis on large motor skills
- simple rhymes and finger plays
- repetition and encouragement
- simple questions and responses

Preschool, 3s & 4s

- an exciting variety of Bible-story tools, including Learning Mats™, *Bible Big Books*™, Jumbo Bible Puzzles™, and Fold-Out Learning Mats™
- guided options in "Let's Get Started" and "For Extra Time"
- side-by-side play
- age-appropriate craft ideas that don't require cutting
- simple interaction using pair-shares and assembly lines

Pre-K & K, 5s & 6s

- Bible stories with more depth based on Learning Mats™, *Bible Big Books*™, Jumbo Bible Puzzles™, and Fold-Out Learning Mats™
- more individual choices and independent learning activities
- thought-provoking questions
- more challenging craft activities
- more frequent use of interactive learning

Of course, *every* age level of **Hands-On Bible Curriculum for Toddlers Through 6-Year-Olds** includes

- exciting, easy-to-prepare lessons
- a CD of lively songs that teach
- photocopiable take-home papers to help parents reinforce Bible truths at home
- a solid biblical point in language young children can understand
- memorable five-senses learning carefully tied to the Bible truth
- big, bright, exciting Bible art
- interaction with a puppet friend who learns from the children
- options that allow you to customize each lesson for your class

Choose the age level that most closely matches your students' needs, then teach with confidence, knowing that you're providing the optimum learning environment for the little ones God has entrusted to your care.

How to Use This Book

Welcome to Hands-On Bible Curriculum™

There's nothing more rewarding than helping young children know, love, and follow Jesus Christ. But getting the message across to preschoolers can be a challenge! Five- and 6-year-olds aren't ready to absorb abstract theological concepts, but they can certainly understand that Jesus loves and cares for them.

Hands-On Bible Curriculum™ for Pre-K & K presents simple Bible truths in a fresh, interactive setting that capitalizes on children's need to experience life with all their senses. With *Group's Bible Big Books*™, *Group's Learning Mats*™, and *Group's Jumbo Bible Puzzles*™, you'll help children discover Bible lessons in creative, active ways that will capture their attention and keep them coming back for more.

Each Hands-On Bible Curriculum lesson for Pre-K & K is based on an impor tant Bible story. Each lesson Point distills the Bible story into a simple, memorable Bible truth that 5- and 6-year-olds can understand and experience.

Active Learning: What I Do, I Learn

Group's Hands-On Bible Curriculum uses a unique approach to Christian education called active learning. In each session, children participate in a variety of fun and memorable learning experiences that help them understand one important point.

Research shows that kids remember about 90 percent of what they *do,* but less than 10 percent of what they *hear.* The 5- and 6-year-olds in your class learn best by doing, smelling, tasting, feeling, hearing, and seeing. They need to be actively involved in lively experiences that bring home the lesson's point.

With active learning, the teacher becomes a guide, pointing the way for the learner to discover Bible truths through hands-on experiences. Instead of filling little minds with facts, you'll participate alongside your students in the joy of discovery, then carefully summarize each Bible truth.

Don't be alarmed if your classroom seems a little noisier with active learning! Educators will tell you that children process new information best by interacting with one another. Having quiet and controlled students doesn't necessarily mean your class is a success. A better clue might be seeing happy, involved, excited children moving around the classroom, discovering Bible truths with all their senses.

In order to succeed with active learning, you'll need an attention-getting signal. An attention-getting signal such as flashing the lights or raising your hand will let children know it's time to stop what they're doing and look at you. You'll find instructions for a signal in the "Setting the Stage" section of each lesson. Each week, remind the children of your signal and practice it together. Soon, regaining their attention will become a familiar classroom ritual.

Interactive Learning: Together We Learn Better

From their earliest years, children learn from interacting with people around them. Bolstered by the encouragement of parents and friends, they try, then fail, then try again until they learn to walk, talk, run, write—the list goes on and on. Because children truly want to learn, they keep seeking help from those around them until they master a concept or skill.

Children don't learn in isolation. Interactive learning comes naturally to young children. So why not put its benefits to work in the church?

In Hands-On Bible Curriculum, children work together to discover and explore Bible truths. The interactive Bible lessons also help children learn kindness, patience, and cooperation. As they assume unique roles and participate in group-learning activities, children discover firsthand that church is a place where everyone can belong, and no one is left out.

Like active learning, interactive learning may produce a bit more noise than you're used to. Sometimes you may feel like you've lost control. But you haven't really lost it—you've just allowed the children to take ownership of their learning. With interactive learning, you won't have to prod students to learn—they'll be motivated by the joy of discovery. Try it, you'll like it!

Use the following guidelines to help make interactive learning work for your class:

● **Establish guidelines for acceptable behavior.** Invite the children to help you create classroom rules. Some rules that work well with 5- and 6-year-olds are: Use quiet voices, stay at your workplace, work together, help each other, and say nice words to others. Children will enjoy reminding each other to follow rules they've helped create.

● **Use paired instruction.** Pair up children with similar abilities during activities. When you ask a question, have children ask that question of their partners.

● **Assign specific tasks to individuals working in groups.** When children work in groups of more than two, each child should be assigned a unique and important task. To help children remember their tasks, consider using colored necklaces, headbands, or badges. If you're making sandwiches, for example, children with red badges could be in charge of bread, children with green badges could be in charge of peanut butter, and children with blue badges could be in charge of jelly.

● **Discuss each activity with the children.** Ask children to tell you what they did, and what they liked and didn't like about it. Invite them to share their learning discoveries with you and with other groups. Praise groups that seemed to work together well, and soon other groups will follow their example.

Learning Is an Exciting Adventure!

Let the Holy Spirit be your guide as you teach this quarter of Hands-On Bible Curriculum. With active and interactive learning, your students will enter a whole new world of Bible discovery. They'll be fascinated with *Group's Bible Big Book, rubber stamps,* and other learning materials in the Learning Lab®. And you'll feel good about seeing children enjoy these important Bible lessons.

Sound exciting? Walk through a lesson and discover how Hands-On Bible Curriculum for Pre-K & K will work for you.

The Point

● **The Point contains the one important Bible truth children will learn in each lesson.** Each Point is carefully worded in simple language that 5- and 6-year-olds can easily understand and remember. Each activity reinforces The Point. You can find The Point by looking for the pointing-pencil icon that accompanies The Point each time it occurs in the text.

● **Be sure to repeat The Point as it's written each time it appears.** You may feel you're being redundant, but you're actually helping children remember an important Bible truth. Studies show that people need to hear new information up to 75 times to learn it. Repetition is a good thing—especially for 5- and 6-year-olds. So remember to repeat The Point as you sum up each activity.

The Bible Basis

● **The Bible Basis gives you background information you'll need to teach the lesson.** The first paragraph provides details and background for the lesson's Bible story. Read the Bible story ahead of time to familiarize yourself with key details. The second paragraph tells how the story and Point relate to 5- and 6-year-olds. Use the developmental information in this paragraph to help you anticipate children's responses.

This Lesson at a Glance

● **The Lesson at a Glance chart gives you a quick overview of the lesson and lists supplies you'll need for each activity.** Most of the supplies are items you already have readily available in your home or classroom. Simplify your preparation by choosing which Let's Get Started and For Extra Time activities you'll use. Then gather only the supplies you'll need for those activities and for the main body of the lesson.

● **Take time to familiarize yourself with the Learning Lab items.** Read the *Bible Big Books,* unfold the *Learning Mat,* listen to the *CD,* stamp with the *rubber stamps.* Pray for your 5- and 6-year-olds as you have fun preparing.

Welcome!

● **Your class begins each week with a time to greet children and welcome them to class.** Five- and 6-year-olds love familiar adults, so use your welcoming presence to affirm each child. You can help strengthen developing friendships by encouraging children to welcome each other as well.

● **When you meet the children in your class for the first time, call them by name.** Introduce yourself to parents and let them know you're glad to be teaching their children. Help children make name tags using the patterns provided in Lesson 1. Consider laminating the name tags after the first week so they'll last the entire quarter. Fasten the name tags to children's clothing using tape or safety pins. Children will enjoy wearing name tags they've made themselves, and you'll find yourself referring to the name tags often when you can't quite remember all the children's names.

● **Model Christ's love to your students by bending down to their level when you listen or speak to them.** Be sure to make eye contact, hold a hand, pat a shoulder, and say each child's name sometime during the morning. Take a few moments to find out how each child is feeling before leading children into your first lesson activity.

Let's Get Started

● **Let's Get Started involves children right away in meaningful activities related to the lesson.** Each lesson provides you with several optional activities for children to do as they arrive. You can choose to do one or more of them. These activities prepare children for the lesson they'll be learning and provide them with opportunities for positive social interaction.

● **Set up appropriate areas in your classroom to accommodate each activity.** Let's Get Started activities range from blocks and fine-motor manipulatives, to dramatic play with dress-up clothing and props, to arts and crafts. Allow plenty of space in each activity area for children to have freedom of movement.

Five- and 6-year-olds use dramatic play to try on roles and process what they know and feel about relationships and the world around them. Set out small dishes and cups, a small table, and typical toy kitchen appliances. If your budget is limited, ask a parent to make play furniture out of wood or use sturdy cardboard boxes. Dolls, blankets, and a doll bed are important elements in an early-childhood classroom.

Provide dress-up clothing that represents male and female roles as well as items that reflect children's culture. You can also gather bathrobes and towels to use as Bible-time costumes. Avoid adult pants or other clothing that might cause children to trip and fall. If your church doesn't have a collection of dress-up clothes, consider asking parents or church members to donate old clothes, hats, and purses or briefcases. Dress-up clothes can also be purchased inexpensively at secondhand stores.

If you use tables, make sure they're child-sized. Forcing children to work at adult-sized tables can cause spills, messes, and even accidents. If your church doesn't have child-sized furniture or if you're meeting in a nontraditional space, set up art or manipulative activities on the floor. Trays, shallow boxes, or dish pans can be used to hold the items needed for the lesson. Use masking tape to mark off the area and cover the floor with newspaper or a plastic tablecloth. Consider using crates or cement blocks to hold up an adult-sized table top with legs collapsed.

● **Make Let's Get Started work for your class!** Depending on the number of children and adult helpers you have, set up one, two, or all of the activities. Station an adult at each activity area and run several activities simultaneously, or lead all children in one activity at a time. If you want to move quickly into the Bible-Story Time, pick one Let's Get Started activity. If you often have latecomers, plan to use more activities.

● **Always discuss each Let's Get Started activity with the children.** Let's Get Started activities allow children to explore The Point independently in a casual setting. Talking with children about these activities helps them make an important faith connection. For example, 5- and 6-year-olds may love playing at a nature table, but they won't connect it with a loving, creator God without your help. Circulate among the areas to guide activities and direct children's conversation toward the lesson. As you have the opportunity, repeat The Point.

- **Vary the activities you use.** Remember that children learn in different ways. The more senses you can involve, the more children will learn. By including a variety of Let's Get Started activities each quarter, you'll be able to reach children of all learning styles and developmental abilities.

Pick-Up Song

- **Sing the Pick-Up Song when you're ready to move on to the Bible-Story Time.** Singing helps young children make a smooth transition to the next activity. Your Pick-Up Song is "We Will Pick Up," sung to the tune of "London Bridge." Shortly before you start singing, tell children that it's almost time to clean up. If you're uncomfortable with singing, use the *CD* or ask a volunteer to help you. At first children will just listen to the song, but they'll quickly catch on and sing along. Soon, cleaning up the room will become a familiar ritual that children actually enjoy!

Bible-Story Time

- **Introduce and review the attention-getting signal.** Attention-getting signals help you stay in control. Use the signal described in the lessons to let children know it's time to stop what they're doing and look at you.
- **Use "Setting the Stage" to formally introduce The Point and set up the Bible-story action.** To wrap up Let's Get Started activities, have children tell you what they did and formally connect their experiences to The Point. Then complete the "Setting the Stage" activity to lead children from The Point to the Bible story. Even though The Point is tied to the Bible story, most 5- and 6-year-olds won't make the connection. The summary statement at the end of the activity will help you provide children with a clear transition.
- **Use "Bible Song and Prayer Time" to teach children to love and respect God's Word.** Choose a special Bible to use for this section of the lesson each week. For example, you could use a big black Bible, a red Bible, or a Bible with gold leaf pages. These special characteristics will make Bible time memorable for the children. Even though you'll be using *Group's Bible Big Book, Learning Mat,* or *Jumbo Bible Puzzle* to tell the Bible story, be sure to tell children that the story comes from the Bible, God's Word. The Bible Song provided in the lesson and on the *CD* will prepare children to focus on the Bible story.
- **Tell the Bible story with enthusiasm.** Read the Bible story and practice telling it before class. If you'll be using the *CD* to tell the story, listen to it ahead of time. Think about voice changes, gestures and motions, and eye contact. Refer to the Teacher Tips in the Teacher Guide to help you.

Use questions in the Teacher Guide to draw children into discussions and help them focus on the Bible story. Invite children to help you tell the Bible story if they already know it. Listen to children's questions and responses, but don't let them steer you too far away from the story.

To refocus children when they become distracted, use a child's name and ask a direct question. You might say, "Cody, how do you think Joseph was feeling when his brothers threw him in the pit?"

- **Move on to "Do the Bible Story" quickly.** Most 5- and 6-year-olds have a five- to 10-minute attention span. After they've been sitting for "Hear the

Bible Story," they'll be ready to get up and move around. The "Do the Bible Story" section lets them jump up and wear out the wiggles without wiggling away from the lesson!

Practicing The Point

● **Practicing The Point lets children practice and teach what they've learned.** In this section, children interact with a puppet friend about The Point. You can use Pockets the Kangaroo, available from Group Publishing, or any puppet of your choice. You can even make your own kangaroo puppet. Pockets is energetic and friendly. She truly wants to understand The Point but often needs to have it explained a few times before she gets it right.

You'll be amazed to discover how much your children have learned as they share the lesson with Pockets. Even children who are shy around adults will open up to Pockets. After several weeks, children will begin to expect Pockets' regular visits and will be eager to set her straight.

For a change of pace, try one of the following ideas for bringing Pockets into other parts of the lesson.
- Have Pockets greet children as they arrive.
- Have children tell the Bible story to Pockets.
- Have Pockets participate in games or other activities.
- Have Pockets ask questions to draw out shy children.
- Have Pockets give the attention-getting signal.
- Have Pockets encourage disruptive children to quiet down.
- Use Pockets to snuggle or hug children.

You can purchase Pockets in your local Christian bookstore or directly from Group Publishing by calling 1-800-447-1070.

Closing

● **The closing activity gives you an opportunity to repeat The Point once more and wrap up the class session.** As you complete the closing activity, encourage children to say The Point with you. Encourage them to share The Point with their families when they go home.

For Extra Time

● **If you have a long class period or simply want to add variety to your lessons, try one of the For Extra Time activities.** For Extra Time activities include learning games, crafts, and snacks related to the lesson, as well as suggestions to enhance each lesson's story picture. Most of these ideas could also be used in the Let's Get Started section of the lesson. Each For Extra Time activity lists the supplies you'll need.

Today I Learned . . .

● **The photocopiable "Today I Learned . . ." handout helps parents and children interact about the lesson.** Each handout includes a verse to learn, family activity ideas, a story picture, and an "Ask Me . . ." section with questions for parents to ask their children about the lesson. Encourage parents to use the handout to help them reinforce what their children are learning at church.

Understanding Your 5- and 6-Year-Olds

Physical Development

- Developing fine motor skills.
- Most can use scissors and color within the lines.
- Developing hand-eye coordination; can copy patterns, handle paste or glue, and tie shoes.

Emotional Development

- Proud of their accomplishments.
- Have their feelings hurt easily.
- Beginning to gain self-confidence.

Social Development

- Learning to share and cooperate.
- Can understand and follow rules.
- Enjoy extensive dramatic play.
- Eager to please teachers and parents.

Mental Development

- Can listen to and create stories.
- Can distinguish between real and pretend.
- Need simple directions—understand one step at a time.

Spiritual Development

- Understand that God made them.
- Trust that God loves them.
- Beginning to develop a sense of conscience.

Dear Parent,

I'm so glad to be your child's teacher this quarter. With our Hands-On Bible Curriculum™, your child will look at the Bible in a whole new way.

For the next 13 weeks, 5- and 6-year-olds will experience the excitement of Jesus' birth, learn what Jesus did as he grew up, and discover that Jesus is always with us today. Using active- and interactive-learning methods and exciting storytelling tools such as *Group's Bible Big Books*™ and *Group's Learning Mat*™, we'll help children discover, understand, and apply God's Word.

Our Hands-On Bible Curriculum welcomes you to play an important part in what your child learns. **Each week when you pick up your child, you'll receive a "Today I Learned..." handout.** "Today I Learned..." tells you what we did in class and provides you with questions and activities to help you reinforce your child's Bible lesson at home.

Let me encourage you to use the "Today I Learned..." handout regularly; it's a great tool for reinforcing Bible truths and promoting positive, healthy communication in your family.

Sincerely,

Jesus' Birth

Through hundreds of years of suffering, captivity, and persecution, the Hebrews waited in hope of God's promised Messiah proclaimed by the prophets. "Be strong. Don't be afraid. Look, your God will come...he will save you" (Isaiah 35:4). Yet who would have thought God would send a mere infant to save humanity from its sins? Before Jesus was born, Mary and Elizabeth knew this baby was a special gift from God. Even the shepherds who worshiped at the lowly manger bed understood the significance of the miraculous infant. And the wise men who traveled from the East came seeking a baby who would be king. All these people knew that this child, born in Bethlehem, would save people from their sins.

Most 5- and 6-year-olds eagerly make Christmas lists, detailing the toys and gadgets they'd like to find under the tree. It's important to help them see that God sent the most perfect gift when he sent Jesus to save us from sin. In this module, children will rediscover the true reason for Christmas—the birthday of God's son! The five lessons in this module will begin with the anticipation of God's promised one announced by Isaiah, then lead children through Gabriel's announcement to Mary and Elizabeth and to Jesus' Bethlehem birth. Children will learn about the angels' announcement to the shepherds and the wise men's search for the newborn king. They'll discover the events of Jesus' birth and celebrate the good news that Jesus came to save them.

Five Lessons on Jesus' Birth

Time Stretchers

What's Missing?

Form a circle and spread the *Nativity Kit* figures from the Learning Lab in the middle of the circle. Have children close their eyes while you remove one figure and hide it in your lap or behind your back. Allow children to open their eyes. Start the *egg timer* and have children raise their hands to guess which figure is missing before the sand in the timer runs out. Let the child who guesses correctly share why that character is important to the Christmas story. Then replace the figure and play again.

Bethlehem Barnyard

Form a circle. Have each child think of an animal that might have been in the stable where Jesus was born. Explain that there could have been sheep, donkeys, horses, cows, or chickens. On your signal, have children make the noise their animal would make. As children are creating their "Bethlehem Barnyard," quietly say to a child near you, "Jesus came to save us. Pass it on!" Have that child stop making his or her noise then whisper the message to another student. As the message is passed along, the room will become quiet. After the last child has passed the message to you, have everyone shout, "Jesus came to save us."

Jesus Saves Us

Help children remember that Jesus came to save us, by singing this song to the tune of "Jesus Loves Me" without the *CD*.

Sing

God promised to send his Son
To bring his love to everyone.
Jesus is God's promise true;
He can save both me and you.

Yes, Jesus saves us.
Yes, Jesus saves us.
Yes, Jesus saves us.
He came for everyone.

Remembering God's Word

Each four- or five-week module focuses on a key Bible verse. The key verse for this module is "A Savior has been born to you; he is Christ the Lord" (Luke 2:11b).

This module's key verse will teach children that Jesus came to save us. Have fun using these ideas any time during the lessons on Jesus' birth.

Echo Song

Gather children and read the key verse to them. Explain that Jesus is our Savior—God's Son who was sent to save us from sin. Then say the verse and have children repeat it. Form two groups and lead children in singing this echo song to the tune of "Frère Jacques." Have Group 2 echo Group 1 in words and motions.

Sing

Baby Jesus *(rock small baby),*
Baby Jesus *(rock small baby),*
Born today *(set imaginary baby in crib/manger),*
Born today *(set imaginary baby in crib/manger),*
In the town of David *(point to something far away),*
In the town of David *(point to something far away),*
Came to save *(hug a friend),*
Came to save. *(Hug a friend.)*

Baby Jesus *(rock baby in arms),*
Baby Jesus *(rock baby in arms),*
God's own Son *(point to heaven),*
God's own Son *(point to heaven),*
Born on earth to save us *(extend arms to heaven),*
Born on earth to save us *(extend arms to heaven),*
Everyone, everyone. *(Everyone make large circle with arms.)*

Lead children in saying the key verse once more.

Rescue Mission

Read Luke 2:11b aloud and have children repeat it after you. Say: **We're going to play a game where you'll have a chance to save others.** Choose one child to be "It" and another child to be the Rescue Train leader. **It will tag as many of you as possible. If you're tagged, freeze right where you are. Meanwhile, the Rescue Train will be coming around to save you! If the Rescue Train leader tags you, link arms and join the Rescue Train. You'll get to help save other frozen children. We'll play until everyone has joined the Rescue Train. Ready? Go!**

When everyone (except It) has joined the Rescue Train, have them link arms with It and sit down together. Read the key verse again and say: **Jesus was born to save us from the bad things we do. We call those things sin. Jesus came to rescue us from sin!** Have children join hands and repeat the verse after you.

Story Enhancements

Make Bible stories come alive in your classroom by bringing in Bible costumes, setting out sensory items that fit with the story, or creating exciting bulletin boards. When children learn with their five senses as well as with their hearts and minds, lessons come alive and children remember them. Each week, bring in one or more of the following items to help involve and motivate children in the Bible lessons they'll be learning. The following ideas will help get you started.

✔ Make a versatile bulletin board to last your entire module. Add a new item each week to hold your students' interest. Begin by covering the bulletin board with newsprint. Then add construction paper letters that spell out "Happy Birthday, Jesus!" across the top.

Lesson 1

● Bring in binoculars for children to use. Talk about how binoculars make far away things seem close up. Tell children that just as the binoculars help us see things that are far away, God helped his people know about the future by telling Isaiah about Jesus.

● Have children cut out balloon shapes from brightly colored construction paper and write their names on them. Then help children tape a length of colored ribbon to their balloons and staple them to the bulletin board. Talk about the celebration you're preparing for!

Lesson 2

● Bring in a blank cassette tape and a tape recorder. Let children take turns singing and recording praise songs to God. Tell children that Mary and Elizabeth praised God for his plan for them. They rejoiced because they were part of God's plan to bring Jesus to save us.

● Bring in a tub of damp sand, twigs, rocks, and plastic spoons. Explain that Mary traveled from Galilee to the hills of Judea as she went to Elizabeth's. Direct children to make hills in the sand and smooth out a road through the hills for Mary to walk on. Children can place rocks and twigs to complete the scene.

● Have children cut confetti from brightly colored construction paper. Allow each child to glue a handful of the confetti to the bulletin board. Explain that we use confetti to celebrate, and we're excited to celebrate Jesus' birthday!

Lesson 3

● Have each child bring in a baby picture. Arrange pictures on a table for children to see. Compare different pictures and see how each child has grown. Remind children that Jesus was once a baby, too.

● Bring in baby foods such as baby teething biscuits, cereal, and jars of fruit for children to taste. Also provide baby items such as powder and lotion for children to smell and use on their hands and arms.

● Have children color newsprint then cut it into thin strips. Show them how to curl the strips around pencils or markers to make curly streamers. Help them staple the streamers around the bulletin board.

Lesson 4

● Tell children that shepherds watched over goats as well as sheep! The goats provided milk for the shepherds and their families. Cheese and kefir (yogurt-like food) were made from the milk curds. Bring in cheese, cottage cheese, and yogurt for children to taste.

● Bring in items made from different types of wool. Have children feel the items and discover how sheep provide warm clothes for us. Discuss how the shepherds had an important job to do as they watched the sheep.

● Give children small, wrapped candy canes and narrow ribbon. Let them wrap ribbon around the candy canes to make shepherds' staffs. Staple the staffs to the balloon ribbons on the bulletin board.

Lesson 5

● Bring in spices such as ginger, cinnamon sticks, whole cloves, and nutmeg to smell. Explain that in Jesus' time, spices were used not only to season food, but also to heal.

● Set out several heavy items and explain that gold would have been heavy for the wise men to take on such a long trip. Talk about what a special gift that was!

● Bring in different-sized squares of wrapping paper. Allow children to fold the paper around scraps of cardboard, then decorate the "gifts" with ribbon, and add their names to gift tags. Help children staple their gifts to the bulletin board as gifts to Jesus.

Jesus: God's Promise

The Bible Basis

Isaiah 11:1-6; 35:3-10. God tells Isaiah that a Savior will come.

Isaiah prophesied during a troubled time in Israel's history. The northern kingdom had fallen, and Judah was under attack. God's people must have felt that peace would never come. That's why Isaiah's words about a Savior brought such hope! In the throes of war, Israel heard of a deliverer—one who would bring peace, justice, healing, and victory to its wounded people. God's message brought the hope of a future to those who'd given up.

Children sometimes lose hope just as the Israelites did. In our world today, kids encounter domestic violence, drug abuse, unsafe neighborhoods, unstable homes, and graphic violence and terrorism on television. Yet we, too, can rejoice and have hope because Jesus came to save us from the sin that surrounds us. By sharing that joy with 5- and 6-year-olds, we can give them a powerful sense of hope that will help them cope with a troubled world. Use this lesson to remind children that they can be happy knowing that Jesus came to save them.

Getting the Point

✏ **We're happy that Jesus came to save us.**

It's important to say The Point just as it's written in each activity. Repeating The Point over and over will help the children remember it and apply it to their lives.

Children will
● learn of Isaiah's message from God,
● tell why they're happy that Jesus came to save us,
● understand the importance of Jesus' birth, and
● share God's promise with Pockets.

● **The Point**

This Lesson at a Glance

Before the lesson, collect the necessary items for the activities you plan to use. Refer to the Classroom Supplies and Learning Lab Supplies columns to determine what you'll need. Remember to make photocopies of the "Today I Learned..." handout (p. 32) to send home with your children.

Section	Minutes	What Children Will Do	Classroom Supplies	Learning Lab Supplies
Welcome Time	up to 5	**Welcome!**—Receive name tags and be greeted by the teacher.	"Star Name Tags" handouts (p. 30), markers, pins or tape	
Let's Get Started — Direct children to one or more of the Let's Get Started activities until everyone arrives.	up to 10	**Option 1: Lion and Lamb Puppets**—Make puppets to illustrate Isaiah's prophecy.	"Lion and Lamb" handouts (p. 31), paper lunch sacks, glue sticks, markers, newspapers	Springfill
	up to 10	**Option 2: A Stable Home**—Prepare the Learning Mat stable for Jesus' arrival.	Brown crayons, cotton balls, glue, gray yarn	Learning Mat: Jesus' Birth, springfill, Sheep and Donkey Nativity Kit figures
	up to 10	**Option 3: A Special Gift**—Decorate a gift box for use later in the lesson.	Large box, squares of gift wrap, scissors, glue, ribbon, markers	Angel stamp and ink pad
Pick-Up Song	up to 5	**We Will Pick Up**—Sing a song as they pick up toys and gather for Bible-Story Time.	CD player	CD: "We Will Pick Up" (track 2)
Bible-Story Time	up to 5	**Setting the Stage**—Play Tag using lion and lamb puppets.	Lion and lamb puppets from Option 1	CD: "God's Book" (track 3), angel stamp and ink pad
	up to 5	**Bible Song and Prayer Time**—Sing a song, bring out the Bible, and pray together.	Bible, construction paper, scissors, basket or box, CD player	
	up to 10	**Hear the Bible Story**—Talk about God's promise of a Savior in Isaiah 11:1-6; 35:3-10.	Bible, lion and lamb puppets from Option 1	
	up to 10	**Do the Bible Story**—Sing a song and play a game to experience the joy of Jesus' birth.		
Practicing the Point	up to 5	**Lions' Roar!**—Teach Pockets about God's promise to send Jesus.	Pockets the Kangaroo, lion and lamb puppets from Option 1	
Closing	up to 5	**The Greatest Gift**—Share reasons why they're glad Jesus came to save us.	Gift Box from Option 3, Life Savers candies	
For Extra Time		For extra-time ideas and supplies, see page 29.		

Jesus came to save us.

Welcome Time

Welcome! (up to 5 minutes)

● Bend down to make eye contact with children as they arrive.
● Greet each child individually with an enthusiastic smile.
● Thank each child for coming to class today.
● Say: **Today we're going to learn that  we're happy that Jesus came to save us.**

● Give each child a photocopy of a "Star" name tag from page 30. Help children write their names on their name tags and pin or tape them to their clothing. You may wish to cover the name tags in clear adhesive paper so that name tags will last for the entire module.
● Direct the children to the Let's Get Started activities you've set up.

● **The Point**

Let's Get Started

Set up one or more of the following activities for children to do as they arrive. After you greet each child, invite him or her to choose an activity.

Circulate among the children to offer help as needed and direct children's conversation toward today's lesson. Ask questions such as "What's the best news you've ever heard?" or "Has anyone ever saved you from a scary situation?"

OPTION 1: Lion and Lamb Puppets (up to 10 minutes)

Before class, make several photocopies of the "Lion and Lamb" handout (p. 31). Cut apart the lion and lamb faces and place them in two separate piles. You'll need one puppet for each student and approximately the same number of lions and lambs.

Cover a table with newspapers and set out the handouts, paper lunch sacks, *springfill*, markers, and glue sticks. Let children choose to make a lion or lamb puppet. Have each child use markers and *springfill* to decorate a puppet face, then glue the face to the bottom of a lunch sack. Show children how to use the puppets.

As children work, ask them what would happen if lions and lambs lived in the same place. (They wouldn't get along peacefully!) Tell children that Jesus came to show us God's love and to bring peace. That's why  we're happy that Jesus came to save us.

● **The Point**

✔ If some students choose not to make puppets, ask volunteers to make extras. You'll need one puppet for each child during "Hear the Bible Story."

OPTION 2: A Stable Home (up to 10 minutes)

Set out the *Learning Mat: Jesus' Birth* and the Sheep and Donkey figures from the *Nativity Kit.* You'll also need *springfill,* glue, cotton balls, gray yarn, and brown crayons. Allow children to glue *springfill* "straw" to the floor of the stable and to the manger. Invite them to color the stable walls on the *Learning Mat.* Have children glue cotton balls on the sheep and gray yarn on the donkey's tail and mane.

While children work, tell them that long ago God promised Jesus would come. Explain that God's people waited hundreds of years for Jesus' birth. Tell children that each week you'll be preparing the *Learning Mat* for the Christmas story and looking forward to Christmas, just as God's people looked forward to Jesus' birth.

TEACHER TIPS

✔ If you want a darker color on your *Learning Mat,* allow children to use markers. However, due to the coated texture of the mat, you'll need to use permanent markers.

OPTION 3: A Special Gift (up to 10 minutes)

Set out a large box, along with scraps of gift wrap, scissors, markers, glue, ribbon, and the *angel stamp and ink pad.* The box needs to be large enough for children to stand in. Allow children to decorate the gift box creatively in a patchwork style. Explain that Jesus came as a special gift from God and that's why ● we're happy that Jesus came to save us.

When children have finished decorating, set the box aside for use later in the lesson.

When everyone has arrived and you're ready to move on to the Bible-Story Time, encourage the children to finish what they're doing and get ready to clean up.

If the ink pad is dry, moisten it with three to five drops of water.

Pick-Up Song

We Will Pick Up (up to 5 minutes)

Lead children in singing "We Will Pick Up" (track 2) with the *CD* to the tune of "London Bridge." Encourage children to sing along as they help clean up the room.

You'll be using this song each week to alert children to start picking up. At first, they may need a little encouragement. But after a few weeks, picking up and singing along will become a familiar routine.

If you want to include the names of all the children in your class, sing the song without the *CD* and repeat the naming section. If you choose to use the *CD,* vary the names you use each week.

Sing

We will pick up all our toys,
All our toys, all our toys.
We will pick up all our toys
And put them all away.

I see (name) picking up,
Picking up, picking up.
I see (name) picking up
And putting toys away.

(Repeat.)

Bible-Story Time

Setting the Stage (up to 5 minutes)

Tell the children you'll clap your hands to get their attention. Explain that when you clap, children are to stop what they're doing, raise their hands, and focus on you. Practice this signal a few times. Encourage children to respond quickly so you'll have time for all the fun activities you've planned.

Give each child a lion or lamb puppet from Option 1. Send the lions to one side of the room and the lambs to the other. Ask:

● **Do these two animals get along very well? Explain.** (No, lions eat lambs; no, lambs are afraid of lions.)

● **What might happen if they were near each other?** (The lambs would all get eaten; the lambs would all run away; it would be scary!)

Say: **You're right! These animals don't get along at all! Let's play a game to show what might happen if they were together. When I say "Go!" you lions chase the lambs by taking teeny, tiny steps. Remember to roar while you're chasing them! The lambs will run away by taking giant steps. Lambs, remember to say "Baaaa" while you're escaping! If a lamb gets tagged by a lion, he or she must come sit against this wall and wait for the game to end. Ready? Go!**

Be sure children travel around the room as you've told them to and play gently. When the last lamb has been tagged, have children switch puppets and play again. Then have the lions sit on one side of the room and the lambs on the other.

Say: **These animals are natural enemies. But the Bible tells us that Jesus can help everyone be at peace with each other—even lions and lambs. When we have Jesus' love in our hearts, we can even love our enemies. To see how nice this would be, let's have each lion come and find a lamb partner to sit with while we sing and pray.**

Have children form lion and lamb pairs before you move on to the next activity. If you have an uneven number of children in your class, form one trio.

Bible Song and Prayer Time (up to 5 minutes)

Before class, make surprise cards for this activity by cutting construction paper into 2×6-inch slips. Prepare a surprise card for each child plus a few extras for visitors. Fold the cards in half, then stamp the *angel stamp* inside one of the surprise cards. Mark Isaiah 11:1-6; 35:3-10 in the Bible you'll be using.

Jesus came to save us.

✔ Choose a Bible you'll use for this section of the lesson each week. A children's Bible or an easy-to-understand translation, such as the New Century Version, works best. Some of the children in your class may be reading. If children can understand the words in the Bible, they'll have more interest in reading it—and they'll learn more from it.

Have the children sit in a circle. Say: **Each week when we come to our circle for our Bible Story, I'll choose someone to be the Bible person. The Bible person will bring me the Bible marked with our Bible story for that week. Before I choose today's Bible person, let's learn our Bible song. As we sing, I'll pass out the surprise cards. Don't look inside your card until the song is over.**

Lead children in singing "God's Book" (track 3) with the *CD* to the tune of "Old MacDonald Had a Farm." As you sing, pass out the folded surprise cards. If you want to include the names of all the children in your class, sing the song without the *CD* and repeat the naming section. If you choose to use the *CD*, vary the names you use each week.

Sing

Now it's time to read God's Book
And hear a Bible story.
It's fun to be here with my
    friends
And hear a Bible story.

(Name)**'s here.**
(Name)**'s here.**
Here is (name).
Here is (name).
**Now it's time to read God's Book
And hear a Bible story.**

Now it's time to read God's Book
And hear a Bible story.
It's fun to be here with my
    friends
And hear a Bible story.

(Name)**'s here.**
(Name)**'s here.**
Here is (name).
Here is (name).
**Now it's time to read God's Book
And hear a Bible story.**

After the song, say: **You may look inside your surprise cards. The person who has the angel stamped inside his or her card will be our Bible person for today.**

Identify the Bible person, then have the rest of the children clap for him or her. Ask the Bible person to bring you the Bible. Help the Bible person open the Bible to the marked place and show the children where your story comes from. Then have the Bible person sit down.

Say: (Name) **was our special Bible person today. Each week we'll have only one special Bible person, but each one of you is a special part of our class! Today we're all learning that** 🔘 **we're glad Jesus came to save us.**

🔘 **The Point**

Let's say a special prayer now and ask God to help us learn why Jesus came to save us. I'll pass around this basket. When the basket comes to you, put your surprise card in it and say, "God, thank you for sending Jesus to save us."

Pass around the basket or box. When you've collected everyone's surprise card, set the basket aside and pick up the Bible. Lead children in this prayer: **God, thank you for the Bible and all the stories in it. Teach us today that** 🔘 **we're glad Jesus came to save us. In Jesus' name, amen.**

🔘 **The Point**

Jesus came to save us.

Children should still have their lion and lamb puppets from "Setting the Stage." Form a circle and say: **Long ago, when God first made the world, everything was good and beautiful and peaceful. But sin came into the world when Adam and Eve disobeyed God. God's perfect world was ruined.** Ask:

● **What is sin?** (Disobeying; doing bad things; not being nice.)

● **What kinds of bad things go on in our world today?** (People hurt each other; people get sick; things aren't fair; people are mean sometimes.)

Say: **Those things are all because of sin! When sin entered the world, people started doing bad, mean things. God's people did bad things—they worshiped idols and disobeyed God.** Ask:

● **How do you think God felt when his people sinned?** (Sad; mad; upset; not good.)

Say: **That's right. So finally, God let an army from Assyria fight against the Israelites, tear down their cities, burn their houses, and make them slaves. God scattered his people all over the country. Let's scatter out like the Israelites.** Have children scatter all over the room, away from each other. Ask:

● **What would it be like to live far away from your friends and family?** (Yucky; lonely; boring; scary.)

Say: **When the Israelites scattered, it became easy for other nations to take over. Soon their land was under attack! That must have been scary! The people longed for God to save them from their enemies, even though they had sinned. So God told Isaiah, a prophet, that he would send a Savior—someone to forgive his people for their sins and bring them back together.**

Let's gather our lambs back together. Have lambs form a circle near you. **The Bible tells us that when the Savior comes, he'll save everyone who believes in God!** Read John 10:16 aloud from an easy-to-understand version of the Bible. Ask:

● **What do you think God means by "other sheep"?** (Other people; people from other countries; people from all over the world.)

Say: **Yes! Jesus wants everyone to come to him so he can take away their sins. Lambs, go find a lion partner and bring him or her back to our circle to sit with you.** When everyone is back together, say: **God told them what life would be like when their Savior came.** Read Isaiah 35:3-10 aloud from an easy-to-understand version of the Bible. Then ask:

● **What would life be like when the Savior came?** (Good; happy; fun; exciting; wonderful.)

● **How do you think the Israelites felt when they heard that?** (Excited; happy; glad.)

● **When do you think they wanted the Savior to come?** (Now; right away; soon.)

Say: **Well, God's people had to wait 700 long, long years for the Savior to come. And when he came, do you know who that Savior was?** Pause for children to respond. **It was Jesus! That's why ⬤ we're happy that Jesus**   ⬤ **The Point**
came to save us! When we ask Jesus to forgive us, he'll take away all the bad things in our hearts and give us peace and joy. When we're filled with Jesus' love, we can be at peace with everyone—even our enemies.

Since our lions and lambs aren't enemies anymore, it's safe to put them away together so we can play a game.

Collect the lion and lamb puppets and put them out of sight.

Do the Bible Story (up to 10 minutes)

Say: **Jesus came to save us from sin. And he wants everyone in the whole world to accept his forgiveness. Let's play a game to see what that's like.**

Choose a child to be "It" and have everyone else scatter around the room and sit down. Sing the following song with It to the tune of the bunny hop. This song is not on the *CD*. If you're not familiar with the bunny hop song, make up your own tune or simply say it as a rhyme.

Jesus came to save us (*put one foot out to the side, then bring it back in*)
And take away our sin. (*Put other foot out to the side, then bring it back in.*)
He can give you joy (*hop once forward, then once backward*)
And make you clean within. (*Hop forward on each word toward another child.*)

Have It travel to another student on the last line and take that child's hand. Then have It hold onto the waist of the other child, who is now It and may travel to another student. Continue until everyone has had a turn to be It and all children are lined up together. Then have children form a circle.

Say: **God sent Jesus to save us from sin. God wants all of us to ask forgiveness for our sins so we can be part of God's family and live forever with God in heaven.** ● **We are happy that Jesus came to save us. Let's tell Pockets about God's promise by using our lion and lamb puppets again.**

● **The Point**

Practicing the Point

Lions' Roar! (up to 5 minutes)

Distribute the lamb and lion puppets. Bring out Pockets the Kangaroo and go through the following puppet script. When you finish the script, put Pockets away and out of sight.

Direct children to put on the puppets and happily roar and "baaaa" until Pockets appears.

Lions' Roar!

PUPPET SCRIPT

Pockets: What's all the noise? (Sees lions and is frightened.) Are those LIONS?

Teacher: Don't be afraid, Pockets! Yes, those are lions and lambs!

(Continued)

Jesus came to save us.

Pockets: Lions and lambs—together! Hey, you lambs better run away before those lions eat you! Shoo! Go on, shoo! I'm afraid of lions—why aren't these lambs afraid?

Teacher: Well, you don't have to be afraid of these lions! These are puppets! We're celebrating God's promise!

Pockets: What's that?

Teacher: Today we learned about a very special promise God made to Isaiah and to all his people. Who can tell Pockets about God's promise?

(Allow children to share what they've learned about God's promise that Jesus came to save us.)

Pockets: Oh, I know about Jesus. My mom told me about him! She said all creation—everything God made—looked forward to Jesus' coming!

Teacher: What else did your mom say?

Pockets: Well, she said Jesus came to save us from sin and make us clean inside so we can live in heaven with him.

Teacher: That's right, Pockets! Today we're celebrating because ⬤ we're happy that Jesus came to save us. And we can share that happiness with others by telling them about God's promise!

Pockets: I want to celebrate, too! (Sings and dances as she leaves.) Let the lions roar, celebrate some more! God's promises are true. He takes care of me and you! Goodbye, everyone!

⬤ **The Point**

TODAY I LEARNED . . .

We believe that Christian education extends beyond the classroom into the home. Photocopy the "Today I Learned . . ." handout (p. 32) for this week and send it home with your children. Encourage parents to use the handout to plan meaningful family activities to reinforce this week's topic. Follow up the "Today I Learned . . ." activities next week by asking children what their families did.

Closing

The Greatest Gift (up to 5 minutes)

Form a circle and place the Gift Box from Option 3 in the center of the circle. Place a bowl of Life Savers candies in the box. Say: **Because God sent Jesus, we can have a new life with God. You might say that Jesus is our lifesaver! Let's share some reasons why ⬤ we're happy that Jesus came to save us.**

⬤ **The Point**

Jesus came to save us.

Have children take turns standing in the box, taking a candy, and sharing a reason they're happy Jesus came to save us. When each person has shared, pray: **Dear God, thank you for sending Jesus to save us and give us new life. Thank you for loving us and wanting us to be with you forever. In Jesus' name, amen.**

For Extra Time

If you have a long class time or want to add additional elements to your lesson, try one of the following activities.

LIVELY LEARNING: Lifesavers!

Form pairs and have children line up opposite the Gift Box. Give the first child in line the *ring*. Send his or her partner to stand beside the Gift Box. Say: **Toss the *ring* into the box. If it looks like you're going to miss, your partner will catch the *ring* and put it in the box for you. Once your partner has saved you by catching the *ring*, hold up your arms and say, "I'm happy that Jesus came to save me!" Then switch places with your partner.**

When everyone has had a turn, put the *ring* away and out of sight.

MAKE TO TAKE: Pine Cone Advent Calendars

Give each child a pine cone and several 2-foot lengths of colored ribbon. Allow children to decorate their pine cones with glitter glue. Then help them glue three or four ribbons to the pine cone, so they stream from the top or bottom. Explain that children can tie a knot in the ribbons each day until Christmas to help them prepare for Jesus' birth.

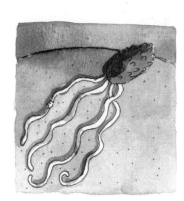

TREAT TO EAT: Lion and Lamb Cookies

You'll need two cookies for each child, plastic knives, white and yellow icing, white and yellow coconut, and raisins. Direct children to ice one cookie with white icing and top it with white coconut to make a lamb. For the lion, have children spread yellow icing and make a mane with yellow coconut. Children may add raisins for eyes.

STORY PICTURE: God's Promise

Give each child a photocopy of the "Today I Learned..." handout from page 32. Set out glue, cotton balls, short lengths of yellow and brown yarn, and crayons. Show children how to glue yarn to the lion's mane and calf's tail. Then have children pull cotton balls apart and glue them to the sheep. After gluing on yarn and cotton balls, children can color the rest of the picture.

Star Name Tags

Jesus came to save us.

Lion and Lamb

Jesus came to save us.

TODAY I LEARNED...

The Point ● We are happy that Jesus came to save us.

Today your child learned that we're happy Jesus came to save us. Children learned that God promised Isaiah and all his people that Jesus would come to save them. Children shared reasons why they're happy Jesus came.

Verse to Learn

"A Savior has been born to you; he is Christ the Lord" (Luke 2:11b).

Ask Me...

● What special promise did God give to Isaiah and to all his people?

● Why are we glad Jesus came?

● How can our family share God's promise with others?

Family Fun

● Make edible lions and lambs by shaping biscuit dough. For each face, flatten and shape one biscuit. Cut thin dough strips to make the lion's mane, then place them around the lion's face. For the lamb, cut small dough triangles for ears. Pull off small bits of dough for lamb's wool and lightly place on face. Make eyes and noses from raisins or red cinnamon candies. After baking the biscuits, your family may wish to share them with a neighbor or friend.

God's Promise (Isaiah 11:1-6; 35:3-10)

Confident Cousins

The Bible Basis

Luke 1:26-56. Mary and Elizabeth celebrate their part in God's plan.

Imagine the shock felt by Mary, a simple teenager engaged to a local carpenter, when the angel Gabriel spoke of her role in the arrival of a Savior. God had certainly blessed her with an important part in his amazing plan! She excitedly made an 80-mile trip to see her cousin, Elizabeth, who was also expecting a miracle baby. The women celebrated God's blessing and praised God for his greatness.

Like Mary, your 5- and 6-year-olds may be surprised to learn that God has a plan for their lives, too. God uses children in many ways—as helpers, encouragers, friends, and teachers to those around them. Use this lesson to teach children that just as Mary and Elizabeth trusted in God's plan, they, too, can trust that Jesus came to save us.

Getting the Point

✏️ **Mary and Elizabeth knew that Jesus came to save us.**

It's important to say The Point just as it's written in each activity. Repeating The Point over and over will help the children remember it and apply it to their lives.

Children will
- learn that Mary and Elizabeth believed in God's promise,
- continue to prepare for Jesus' arrival,
- understand that Mary and Elizabeth were a part of God's plan, and
- teach Pockets that we can share God's promises with others.

✏️ **The Point**

This Lesson at a Glance

Before the lesson, collect the necessary items for the activities you plan to use. Refer to the Classroom Supplies and Learning Lab Supplies columns to determine what you'll need. Remember to make photocopies of the "Today I Learned..." handout (p. 44) to send home with your children.

Section	Minutes	What Children Will Do	Classroom Supplies	Learning Lab Supplies
Welcome Time	up to 5	**Welcome!**—Receive name tags and be greeted by the teacher.	"Star Name Tags" handouts (p. 30), markers, pins or tape	
Let's Get Started Direct children to one or more of the Let's Get Started activities until everyone arrives.	up to 10	**Option 1: Angelic Message Center**—Decorate angels and make special messages for others.	Paper, glitter glue, glue sticks, markers, "Angelic Greeting" handouts (p. 43)	Angel Nativity Kit figure, angel stamp and ink pad
	up to 10	**Option 2: Happy House**—Work together to build Elizabeth's house.	Newspapers, masking tape, paper grocery sacks	
	up to 10	**Option 3: Bethlehem Builders**—Add the finishing touches to the town of Bethlehem on the Learning Mat.	Construction paper, scissors, glue sticks, paper lunch sack	Learning Mat: Jesus' Birth
Pick-Up Song	up to 5	**We Will Pick Up**—Sing a song as they pick up toys and gather for Bible-Story Time.	CD player	CD: "We Will Pick Up" (track 2)
Bible-Story Time	up to 5	**Setting the Stage**—Spread good news without using words.		
	up to 5	**Bible Song and Prayer Time**—Sing a song, bring out the Bible, and pray together.	Bible, construction paper, scissors, basket or box, CD player	CD: "God's Book" (track 3), angel stamp and ink pad
	up to 10	**Hear the Bible Story**—Talk about God's plan for Mary and how she shared the news with Elizabeth, based on Luke 1:26-56.	Bible, cloth or facial tissue, tape, CD player	Mary, Joseph, and Angel Nativity Kit figures; CD: "Joy to the World" (track 4)
	up to 10	**Do the Bible Story**—Search for a clue to a hidden treasure, then share that treasure with others.	Individually wrapped treats, Gift Box from Lesson 1, 3x5 cards	Angel stamp and ink pad
Practicing the Point	up to 5	**Pockets' Good News**—Hear Pockets share a good news promise.	Pockets the Kangaroo, envelope	
Closing	up to 5	**Sunday Best**—Decorate Mary and Joseph to prepare them for Jesus' arrival.	Cinnamon, colored sugar, glue sticks, paper plates	Mary and Joseph Nativity Kit figures
For Extra Time		For extra-time ideas and supplies, see page 42.		

Jesus came to save us.

Welcome Time

Welcome! (up to 5 minutes)

- Bend down to make eye contact with children as they arrive.
- Greet each child individually with an enthusiastic smile.
- Thank each child for coming to class today.
- As children arrive, ask them about last week's "Today I Learned..." discussion. Ask questions such as "How did your family share God's promises with others?" and "How did you prepare for Jesus' arrival this week?"
- Say: **Today we're going to learn that 🔵 Mary and Elizabeth knew that Jesus came to save us.**
- Hand out the star name tags children made in the first lesson and help them attach the name tags to their clothing. If some of the name tags were damaged or if some of the children weren't in class that week, have them make new name tags using the photocopiable handout on page 30.
- Direct the children to the Let's Get Started activities you've set up.

🔵 **The Point**

Let's Get Started

Set up one or more of the following activities for children to do as they arrive. After you greet each child, invite him or her to choose an activity.

Circulate among the children to offer help as needed and direct children's conversation toward today's lesson. Ask questions such as "How do you feel when you get good news?" or "What do you do when you hear good news?"

OPTION 1: Angelic Message Center (up to 10 minutes)

Before children arrive, make several photocopies of the "Angelic Greeting" handout (p. 43). Set out the Angel figure from the *Nativity Kit,* glitter glue, glue sticks, paper, markers, and the *angel stamp and ink pad.* Allow children to help spread glitter glue over the figure. Explain that the angel was God's special messenger. Then have children cut out cards on the handouts, fold on the dotted lines, and use the glitter glue, *angel stamp and ink pad,* and markers to make cards to use for special Christmas messages of their own. As children work, tell them that in today's story an angel brought an important message to someone. Encourage children to use their cards to tell someone about Jesus' birth. Set the angel aside for use with the *Learning Mat.*

OPTION 2: Happy House (up to 10 minutes)

Set out paper grocery sacks, newspapers, and masking tape and direct children to set up an assembly line to make blocks for building a house. Have some children be fillers who wad up newspapers and stuff them in the sacks. Others can be folders who fold the top of the bags down twice, then tape them. When children have made a good supply of blocks, allow them to build a house and tape the bricks together. Tell them that this is a happy house because of the good news God sent to the people who lived there. Explain

Jesus came to save us.

The Point

that two women, 🖊 Mary and Elizabeth, knew that Jesus came to save us. You'll use the house in "Hear the Bible Story."

☐ **OPTION 3: Bethlehem Builders (up to 10 minutes)**

Before class, cut sheets of purple, blue, and gray construction paper into small pieces and put them in a paper lunch sack.

Lay the *Learning Mat: Jesus' Birth* on the floor and place glue sticks and the sack of paper pieces nearby. Demonstrate how to glue the paper pieces mosaic-style onto the buildings in the town of Bethlehem. Help them work to fill in as much of the town as possible. As children are working, tell them that today's story is about a special woman who would soon make an important visit to Bethlehem. Explain that she knew that Jesus was coming to save us.

When everyone has arrived and you're ready to move on to the Bible-Story Time, encourage the children to finish what they're doing and get ready to clean up.

Pick-Up Song

We Will Pick Up (up to 5 minutes)

Lead children in singing "We Will Pick Up" (track 2) with the *CD* to the tune of "London Bridge." Encourage the children to sing along as they help clean up the room.

If you want to include the names of all the children in your class, sing the song without the *CD* and repeat the naming section. If you choose to use the *CD*, vary the names you use each week.

Sing

We will pick up all our toys,
All our toys, all our toys.
We will pick up all our toys
And put them all away.

I see (name) picking up,
Picking up, picking up.
I see (name) picking up
And putting toys away.

(Repeat.)

Bible-Story Time

Setting the Stage (up to 5 minutes)

Tell the children you'll clap your hands to get their attention. Explain that when you clap, children are to stop what they're doing, raise their hands, and focus on you. Practice this signal a few times. Encourage children to respond quickly so you'll have time for all the fun activities you've planned.

Form two groups and send each one to an opposite side of the room. Say: **Since today's story is about a special message, let's practice sending special messages to each other. I'll whisper a Christmas message to each group. Then you'll get to pass your message to the other group . . . without using any words!**

Huddle with Group 1 and whisper a Christmas message such as "Jesus is God's Son," "Jesus was born in Bethlehem," or "Jesus came to save us." Then give them a few seconds to come up with a way to deliver that message, such as acting it out or drawing a picture about it. After Group 1 has delivered its message, repeat the process with Group 2. Then have children form a circle. Ask:

● **What was it like to tell that good news?** (Fun; hard; silly.)

● **What other good news have you heard lately?** (We're going to Disneyland; my sister won an award; my mom's having a baby.)

● **What do you like to do when you hear good news?** (Tell people; share it; jump up and down.)

Say: **Today we'll learn what a woman named Mary did when she heard some extra-good news! God sent her the good news in a special way. You'll see that** ● **Mary and Elizabeth knew that Jesus came to save us.**

● **The Point**

Bible Song and Prayer Time (up to 5 minutes)

Before class, make surprise cards for this activity by cutting construction paper into 2×6-inch slips. Prepare a surprise card for each child plus a few extras for visitors. Fold the cards in half, then stamp the *angel stamp* inside one of the surprise cards. Mark Luke 1:26-56 in the Bible you'll be using.

Have the children sit in a circle. Say: **Now it's time to choose a Bible person to bring me the Bible marked with today's Bible story. As we sing our Bible song, I'll pass out the surprise cards. Don't look inside your card until the song is over.**

Lead children in singing "God's Book" (track 3) with the *CD* to the tune of "Old MacDonald Had a Farm." As you sing, pass out the folded surprise cards. If you want to include the names of all the children in your class, sing the song without the *CD* and repeat the naming section. If you choose to use the *CD*, vary the names you use each week.

Sing

Now it's time to read God's Book
And hear a Bible story.
It's fun to be here with my
    friends
And hear a Bible story.

(Name)**'s here.**
(Name)**'s here.**
Here is (name).
Here is (name).
Now it's time to read God's Book
And hear a Bible story.

Now it's time to read God's Book
And hear a Bible story.
It's fun to be here with my
    friends
And hear a Bible story.

(Name)**'s here.**
(Name)**'s here.**
Here is (name).
Here is (name).
Now it's time to read God's Book
And hear a Bible story.

After the song, say: **You may look inside your surprise cards. The person who has the angel stamped inside his or her card will be our Bible person for today.**

Identify the Bible person, then have the rest of the children clap for him or her. Ask the Bible person to bring you the Bible. Help the Bible person open the Bible to the marked place and show the children where your story comes from. Then have the Bible person sit down.

Say: (Name) **was our special Bible person today. Each week we'll have only one special Bible person, but each one of you is a special part of our class! Today we're all learning that** ● **Mary and Elizabeth knew that Jesus came to save us.**

Let's say a special prayer now and ask God to help us learn more about how Jesus came to save us. I'll pass around this basket. When the basket comes to you, put your surprise card in it and say, "God, help me learn about how Jesus came to save us."

Pass around the basket or box. When you've collected everyone's surprise card, set the basket aside and pick up the Bible. Lead children in this prayer: **God, thank you for the Bible and all the stories in it. Teach us today that** ● **Mary and Elizabeth knew that Jesus came to save us, amen.**

Hear the Bible Story (up to 10 minutes)

Hold up the Bible and say: **Our Bible story today comes from the book of Luke in the Bible. In our last Bible story we learned about the promise God gave to Isaiah. And Isaiah told that promise to God's people.** Ask:

● **What was the promise God gave to Isaiah?** (Jesus would come to save us; there would be peace; everyone would get along.)

Say: **God's promise was to send a Savior who would save us from our sins. In our Bible story today, we'll learn more about God's promise to send Jesus.**

Set out the Mary, Joseph, and Angel figures from the *Nativity Kit*. Choose three volunteers and give each one a Nativity figure to hold up during the story. Say: **Our story today is about a woman named Mary.** Point to the figure of Mary. **Mary loved God very much. Let's show how special Mary is by putting a nice shawl around her shoulders.** Choose a volunteer to tape a small piece of cloth or a facial tissue around the figure of Mary. **She was getting ready to marry a carpenter named Joseph. Joseph loved God, too. One day, Mary had a special visitor! An angel came to her house and told her a wonderful message.** Have the child holding the Angel stand near Mary. **The angel told Mary that God had chosen her to be the mother of Jesus! Mary was surprised and excited! Can you show me your surprised and excited expressions?** Pause for children to show you their expressions. **Well, that's how Mary might have looked! She just had to tell someone her wonderful news. So she took a long trip to see her cousin, Elizabeth. Let's help Mary take her long trip.**

Lead the children on a winding journey around the classroom until they arrive at the house from Option 2. Set the figure of Mary in front of the house. If you didn't use Option 2, you can return to your original story area.

Say: **When Mary arrived at Elizabeth's house, she told Elizabeth excitedly what the angel had said. She was going to be Jesus' mother! Elizabeth was extra excited because she was going to have a special**

● **The Point**

● **The Point**

baby, too! The two women celebrated and praised God because  **Mary and Elizabeth knew that Jesus came to save us!** Collect the figures and put them out of sight. Then ask:

● **What did the angel tell Mary?** (That she would be Jesus' mommy; that she was going to have a baby.)

● **How do you think Mary felt when she heard the news?** (Excited; glad; happy.)

Say: **That's right! Mary was excited. I'll bet there was lots of joy in Elizabeth's house that day. We can celebrate, too! Let's sing "Joy to the World" to remind us how happy Mary was that she was going to be Jesus' mommy.**

Sing "Joy to the World" (track 4) with the *CD*.

Sing

Joy to the world! The Lord is come;
Let earth receive her king.
Let every heart prepare him room,
And heaven and nature sing,
And heaven and nature sing,
And heaven, and heaven and nature sing.

(Repeat.)

When the song ends, turn off the CD player and put the *CD* away.

Say: **Mary and Elizabeth praised God because**  **they knew that Jesus came to save us. Mary was happy to share her good news with Elizabeth. In our next activity, you may have a chance to share something terrific with your friends!**

Do the Bible Story (up to 10 minutes)

Before class, place a bag of individually wrapped candies in the Gift Box children made last week. Put the box in an inconspicuous place in the room, such as behind a desk or curtain. Stamp the *angel stamp* on several 3×5 cards and draw a picture of a wrapped gift on one card. You may want to color the picture to look like the box your class decorated last week.

Lay the 3×5 cards in front of you, face down. Say: **This game will give you a chance to be like an angel and bring good things to others. Each card has a picture on it. Most of them are pictures of angels. If you turn over an angel card, give a high five to the person who's sitting on your right. There's one card in here that will give a clue about where to find a treat. If you turn that card over, find the treat and share it with all of us right away. Ready?**

Call children forward one at a time to turn over a card. Be sure each person has a turn, even after the Gift Box card has been found. After each child has turned over a card, ask:

● **Which kind of card did you want to get? Explain.** (An angel card so I could give my friend a high five; the treat card because I like to find things.)

Say: **Mary's good news was even better than getting a treat! She was going to be Jesus' mommy! Mary was excited to share that with Elizabeth.**  **Mary and Elizabeth knew that Jesus came to save us.** It's

● **The Point**

● **The Point**

● **The Point**

Jesus came to save us.

sure nice to share good things! Say, let's share our happy story with Pockets!

Practicing the Point

Pockets' Good News (up to 5 minutes)

Before class tape a small envelope to Pockets' hand.

Bring out Pockets the Kangaroo and go through the following puppet script. When you finish the script, put Pockets away and out of sight.

Pockets' Good News

Puppet Script

Pockets: *(Out of breath.)* Hi, everyone! *(Waves envelope.)* I ran all the way here! I got a card—see, a real card in the mail!

Teacher: Hi, Pockets! That's great! Who's the card from?

Pockets: Oh, that's the best part! It's from my grandmother! She's coming to see me. And she's promised that we'll go shopping, and she'll make cookies and tell me stories!

Teacher: That's wonderful news! When's your grandmother coming?

Pockets: She'll be here in 1...2...3 days—that's a long time.

Teacher: Yes, but sometimes we have to wait for promises. We've been learning about a promise God made long ago. Children, let's share our good news with Pockets. *(Let children tell Pockets about Gabriel's visit to Mary and what he told her.)* Mary was so happy about her good news that she went to share it with Elizabeth. Sharing good news makes us happy!

Pockets: I like that Bible story! I sort of know what Mary felt like.

Teacher: Why is that, Pockets?

Pockets: Well, she had good news and I do, too. She shared it with Elizabeth. I shared my news with you. And we both have to wait on promises!

Teacher: That's right, Pockets.

Pockets: You know, 1...2...3 days isn't very long—I've got to get my room all cleaned up for Grandmother. Did Mary have a lot to do to get ready for Jesus to be born?

Teacher: I imagine so, Pockets.

Pockets: Goodbye, everyone! I'm going to get ready for Grandmother!

Jesus came to save us.

TODAY I LEARNED . . .

We believe that Christian education extends beyond the classroom into the home. Photocopy the "Today I Learned . . ." handout (p. 44) for this week and send it home with your children. Encourage parents to use the handout to plan meaningful family activities to reinforce this week's topic. Follow up the "Today I Learned . . ." activities next week by asking children what their families did.

Closing

Sunday Best (up to 5 minutes)

Set out one-half cup of colored sugar in a bowl and a jar of ground cinnamon. Say: **I'm glad Pockets shared her good news with us! I bet she's home cleaning her room right now—getting ready for her grandmother's visit. We need to get our Nativity figures ready for Jesus' visit, too.**

Run a glue stick over the robes of the Mary and Joseph *Nativity Kit* figures and set each figure on a separate paper plate. Call children up one at a time and allow them to choose which figure they'd like to decorate. Have children sprinkle a pinch of colored sugar on Mary's robe or shake a bit of cinnamon on Joseph's robe. Say: **It's exciting to get these figures ready. It was exciting for Mary and Elizabeth to know that God's promise would soon come true.** As each child comes forward, say: (Name)**, God had a special plan for Joseph and Mary, and God has a special plan for you, too.**

✔ If you have more than 10 children in your class, call students up two at a time to be affirmed.

When each child has been affirmed, close with a prayer similar to this one: **Dear God, thank you for the special way you used Mary and Elizabeth. And thank you that ✏ Mary and Elizabeth knew that Jesus came to save us. Help us learn to serve you in special ways, too. In Jesus' name, amen.**

Allow the glue to dry before putting the figures back in the *Nativity Kit.*

🖊 **The Point**

For Extra Time

If you have a long class time or want to add additional elements to your lesson, try one of the following activities.

LIVELY LEARNING: Angel's Flight

Have kids form a large circle and give each child a paper plate to stand on. Take away one plate and choose one child to be the Angel to stand in the middle of the circle. Tell children that when the Angel says, "Fly, angels, fly," everyone must tiptoe to a different plate. Explain that the Angel will be looking for a plate to stand on as well. The child who can't find another plate is the next Angel. As children are playing, remind them that God sent a messenger angel to tell Mary the good news about Jesus.

MAKE TO TAKE: Angelic Greeting

● **The Point**

Photocopy the "Angelic Greeting" handout from page 43 so you have enough for each child to have one. Have children cut, fold, and decorate the cards to look like the special angel that brought Mary the good news. You may want to help children write a special message to a family member or friend on the inside. As children work, remind them that ● Mary and Elizabeth knew that Jesus came to save us because the angel Gabriel told Mary.

TREAT TO EAT: Edible Map

Before class, add a few drops of green food coloring to a container of white frosting and pour red cinnamon candies into small bowls for children to share.

Set out bowls of colored frosting and give each child a graham cracker and a plastic knife. Have children spread frosting on their crackers, then place two candies at the top corner to represent Galilee and two at the bottom to represent Elizabeth's house. Then have children make Mary's path with a single squiggly line of candies, connecting the two places. As children make their edible maps, encourage them to tell about good news they've shared with friends. Remind children that the best news to share is that Jesus came to save us.

STORY PICTURE: Mary Visits Elizabeth

Give each child a photocopy of the "Today I Learned..." handout from page 44, scraps of material, glue, scissors, and crayons. Direct children to cut out material for Mary's and Elizabeth's clothes and glue them to the picture. Use crayons to color the rest of the picture. Talk about how happy the women were about God's promise.

Jesus came to save us.

Angelic Greeting

Cut out the card and fold the pop-up angel inside.

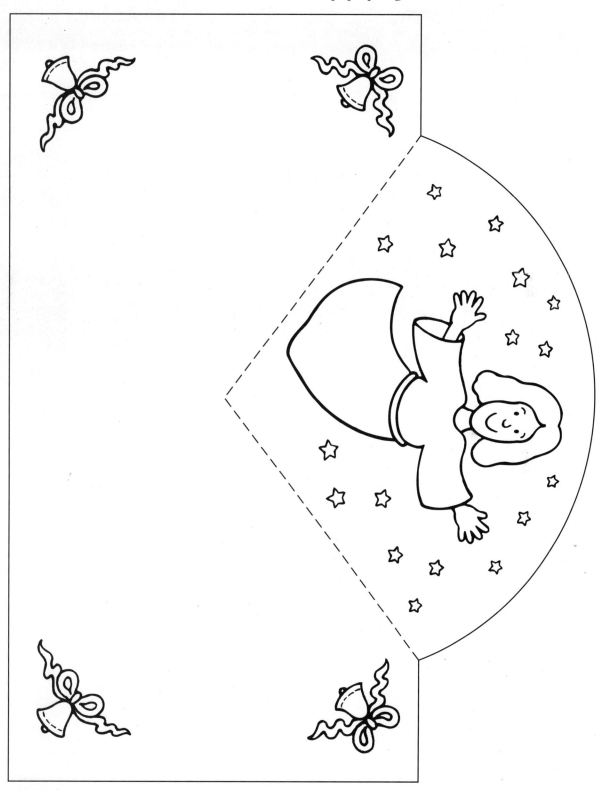

TODAY I LEARNED . . .

The Point ✏ Mary and Elizabeth knew that Jesus came to save us.

LESSON 2

Today your child learned that Mary and Elizabeth knew that Jesus came to save us. Children learned about God's special plan for Mary to be Jesus' mother and that God has a special plan for them. They praised God for his promise in Jesus.

Verse to Learn

"A Savior has been born to you; he is Christ the Lord" (Luke 2:11b).

Ask Me . . .

● What was God's special plan for Mary?
● Who can you tell the good news about Jesus?
● In what ways can our family praise God for sending Jesus to save us?

Family Fun

● Celebrate Jesus' birth by bringing out the family photo album. Share fun memories of the children as babies. Remind each child that he or she is a special gift from God to the family.
● Work together to write a family letter to send with your Christmas greetings. In the letter, share the good news that Jesus came to save us.

Mary Visits Elizabeth (Luke 1:26-56)

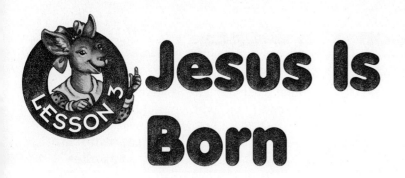

Jesus Is Born

The Bible Basis

Luke 2:1-7. Jesus is born in Bethlehem.

Jesus' humble birth foreshadows a life of human hardship. This divine child, born in a feeding trough, would later walk among lepers, prostitutes, demoniacs, and corrupt tax collectors. He would hang on a cross like a common criminal and bear the sin of the world. And he would willingly give his life to offer us the gifts of forgiveness and eternal life. God's Son was born to die.

Children love giving and receiving gifts, which is why the Christmas season holds so much joy and anticipation for them. Through the story of Jesus' birth, they can learn that Jesus is God's greatest gift to us and that when we celebrate Jesus' birthday, we also celebrate God's love. Use this lesson to teach children that God loved us enough to send his only Son to be our Savior.

Getting the Point

🖊 **Jesus came to save us and was born in Bethlehem.**

It's important to say The Point just as it's written in each activity. Repeating The Point over and over will help the children remember it and apply it to their lives.

Children will
● learn that Jesus was born in a stable in Bethlehem,
● understand that God kept his promise by sending Jesus,
● discover the best gift they can give Jesus, and
● teach Pockets about Jesus' birth.

🖊 **The Point**

This Lesson at a Glance

Before the lesson, collect the necessary items for the activities you plan to use. Refer to the Classroom Supplies and Learning Lab Supplies columns to determine what you'll need. Remember to make photocopies of the "Today I Learned..." handout (p. 56) to send home with your children.

Section	Minutes	What Children Will Do	Classroom Supplies	Learning Lab Supplies
Welcome Time	up to 5	**Welcome!**—Receive name tags and be greeted by the teacher.	"Star Name Tags" handouts (p. 30), markers, pins or tape	
Let's Get Started Direct children to one or more of the Let's Get Started activities until everyone arrives.	up to 10	**Option 1: My Heart**—Make a gift for Jesus.	Colored wrapping paper, stapler, ribbon	
	up to 10	**Option 2: Light Up the Sky!**—Paint a night sky on the Learning Mat to prepare it for today's story.	Clothespins, cotton balls, liquid soap, blue paint, pie tins, newspapers, crayons	Learning Mat: Jesus' Birth
	up to 10	**Option 3: Class Counting**—Make a record of class members.	Paper, pencils, crayons	Ink pad
Pick-Up Song	up to 5	**We Will Pick Up**—Sing a song as they pick up toys and gather for Bible-Story Time.	CD player	CD: "We Will Pick Up" (track 2)
Bible-Story Time	up to 5	**Setting the Stage**—Try to fit in where there's no room.	Masking tape, paper plates	
	up to 5	**Bible Song and Prayer Time**—Sing a song, bring out the Bible, and pray together.	Bible, construction paper, scissors, basket or box, CD player	CD: "God's Book" (track 3), angel stamp and ink pad
	up to 10	**Hear the Bible Story**—Participate in a puppet show about Jesus' birth based on Luke 2:1-7.	Two chairs, blanket, craft sticks, CD player, facial tissue, transparent tape	Nativity Kit figures, Learning Mat: Jesus' Birth, sticky tak, CD: "Away in a Manger" (track 5)
	up to 10	**Do the Bible Story**—Guess what noises Joseph and Mary might have heard in the stable that night, then sing a song to celebrate Jesus' birth.	CD player	CD: "Bethlehem Barnyard" (track 6) and "Baby Jesus" (track 7)
Practicing the Point	up to 5	**No Kangaroo**—Help Pockets learn that everyone can celebrate Jesus' birth.	Pockets the Kangaroo	
Closing	up to 5	**Hearts for Jesus**—Wrap gifts for Jesus and pray.	Hearts from Option 1, wrapping paper, tape, scissors, ribbon	
For Extra Time		For extra-time ideas and supplies, see page 54.		

46 ● Lesson 3   Jesus was born in Bethlehem.

Welcome Time

Welcome! (up to 5 minutes)

- Bend down to make eye contact with children as they arrive.
- Greet each child individually with an enthusiastic smile.
- Thank each child for coming to class today.
- As children arrive, ask them about last week's "Today I Learned..." discussion. Ask questions such as "How did your family celebrate Jesus' birth?" and "What ways did you praise God?"
- Say: **Today we're going to learn that Jesus came to save us and was born in Bethlehem.**
- Hand out the star name tags children made in Lesson 1 and help them attach the name tags to their clothing. If some of the name tags were damaged or if some of the children weren't in class that week, have them make new name tags using the photocopiable handout on page 30.
- Direct the children to the Let's Get Started activities you've set up.

◐ The Point

Let's Get Started

Set up one or more of the following activities for children to do as they arrive. After you greet each child, invite him or her to choose an activity.

Circulate among the children to offer help as needed and direct children's conversation toward today's lesson. Ask questions such as "What's the best gift you've ever received?" or "What gifts does God give to you?"

☐ OPTION 1: My Heart (up to 10 minutes)

Set out 1×9-inch strips of red, green, and gold wrapping paper. Have children work in pairs to make heart ornaments. Demonstrate how to place three strips together and make a loop, then pull each strip to a different length, as shown in the margin. Help each child staple the loop at the bottom, then make a second loop. Have one partner hold the two loops together while the other partner staples them together to make a heart. Show children how to slip a loop of ribbon between two halves of the heart and staple it to make a hanger. Have volunteers make extra heart ornaments for those who choose not to do this activity. As children work, explain that God loves us and sent Jesus to save us. Tell children that ◐ Jesus came to save us and was born in Bethlehem.

◐ The Point

✔ If some children don't choose Option 1, have volunteers make extra hearts so each child has one.

The Point

OPTION 2: Light Up the Sky! (up to 10 minutes)

Cover your work area with newspapers and lay the *Learning Mat: Jesus' Birth* on top. Have children use yellow and white crayons to color in the small stars in the sky. As children are working, pour dark blue or violet paint in pie tins and add a few drops of liquid soap. Make paint daubers by clipping cotton balls to the ends of several clothespins. Show children how to dip their cotton balls in paint then paint over the sky, being careful to avoid the large star in the middle. Explain that today's story tells us that  Jesus came to save us and was born in Bethlehem. Set the finished *Learning Mat* in a warm, sunny place to dry.

OPTION 3: Class Counting (up to 10 minutes)

Before class make a census chart, like the one in the margin. As children come to class, have a helper show them how to write their names in the left-hand column, then write the number of people in their families in the right-hand column. Give children a sheet of paper and instruct them to make a class census. Children may draw a picture, make a thumb print with the *ink pad,* or make a simple crayon mark to represent each member of the class. Explain that in today's story they'll hear about a time when the king ordered that a record be made of all the people in his kingdom.

When everyone has arrived and you're ready to move on to the Bible-Story Time, encourage the children to finish what they're doing and get ready to clean up.

Pick-Up Song

We Will Pick Up (up to 5 minutes)

Lead children in singing "We Will Pick Up" (track 2) with the *CD* to the tune of "London Bridge." Encourage the children to sing along as they help clean up the room.

If you want to include the names of all the children in your class, sing the song without the *CD* and repeat the naming section. If you choose to use the *CD,* vary the names you use each week.

Sing

We will pick up all our toys,
All our toys, all our toys.
We will pick up all our toys
And put them all away.

I see (name) picking up,
Picking up, picking up.
I see (name) picking up
And putting toys away.

(Repeat.)

Jesus was born in Bethlehem.

Bible-Story Time

Setting the Stage (up to 5 minutes)

Tell the children you'll clap your hands to get their attention. Explain that when you clap, children are to stop what they're doing, raise their hands, and focus on you. Encourage children to respond quickly so you'll have time for all the fun activities you've planned.

Before this game, use masking tape to make a large X in the middle of the room. Then put three paper plates at different places around the room. Gather children and say: **When I say "Go," you'll have five seconds to touch a paper plate. When I say "stop," you need to be either on a plate or on the big X. The X is our safety zone. If you're not on a plate or on the X when I say "stop," you're out of the game. Ready? Go!** After five seconds, say: **Stop! Let's make this a little more challenging by taking one of the paper plates away.** Take one plate away and play again. Then remove one more plate before playing again. After you call "stop," gather children together and ask:

● **What was it like to look for a spot to fit into?** (Exciting; it made me nervous; I didn't want to be left out; fun.)

● **What happened when there was no room for you on a plate?** (I knew I could go to the safety zone; I hurried to the X.)

Say: **The safety zone gave everyone a place to go. Our Bible story today is about a time when there wasn't enough room for Mary and Joseph, and it was time for Mary to have her baby! Joseph had to find a safe place—fast! Let's hear about how ◐ Jesus came to save us and was born in Bethlehem.**

◐ The Point

Bible Song and Prayer Time (up to 5 minutes)

Before class, make surprise cards for this activity by cutting construction paper into 2×6-inch slips. Prepare a surprise card for each child plus a few extras for visitors. Fold the cards in half, then stamp the *angel stamp* inside one of the surprise cards. Mark Luke 2:1-7 in the Bible you'll be using.

Have the children sit in a circle. Say: **Now it's time to choose a Bible person to bring me the Bible marked with today's Bible story. As we sing our Bible song, I'll pass out the surprise cards. Don't look inside your card until the song is over.**

Lead children in singing "God's Book" (track 3) with the *CD* to the tune of "Old MacDonald Had a Farm." As you sing, pass out the folded surprise cards. If you want to include the names of all the children in your class, sing the song without the *CD* and repeat the naming section. If you choose to use the *CD*, vary the names you use each week.

Sing

Now it's time to read God's Book	(Name)'s here.
And hear a Bible story.	(Name)'s here.
It's fun to be here with my friends	Here is (name).
And hear a Bible story.	Here is (name).
	Now it's time to read God's Book
	And hear a Bible story.

Now it's time to read God's Book	(Name)'s here.
And hear a Bible story.	(Name)'s here.
It's fun to be here with my	Here is (name).
friends	Here is (name).
And hear a Bible story.	Now it's time to read God's Book
	And hear a Bible story.

After the song, say: **You may look inside your surprise cards. The person who has the angel stamped inside his or her card will be our Bible person for today.**

Identify the Bible person, then have the rest of the children clap for him or her. Ask the Bible person to bring you the Bible. Help the Bible person open the Bible to the marked place and show the children where your story comes from. Then have the Bible person sit down.

Say: **(Name) was our special Bible person today. Each week we'll have only one special Bible person, but each one of you is a special part of our class! Today we're all learning that ⬤ Jesus came to save us and was born in Bethlehem.**

✏️ The Point

Let's say a special prayer now and ask God to help us learn about how Jesus came to save us and was born in Bethlehem. I'll pass around this basket. When the basket comes to you, put your surprise card in it and say, "God, thank you for sending Jesus to save us."

Pass around the basket or box. When you've collected everyone's surprise card, set the basket aside and pick up the Bible. Lead children in this prayer: **God, thank you for the Bible and all the stories in it. Teach us today**

✏️ The Point

that ⬤ Jesus came to save us and was born in Bethlehem, amen.

Hear the Bible Story (up to 10 minutes)

Before this activity, tape the *Learning Mat: Jesus' Birth* to a wall near your story area. Place two chairs in front of the *Learning Mat*. Drape a blanket over the front of the chairs to make them into a puppet stage. Pinch off some of the *sticky tak* and press it onto the back of the Mary, Joseph, and Donkey *Nativity Kit* figures. Then press a craft stick into the *sticky tak* on the back of each figure to make stick puppets. Secretly give the Baby Jesus figure to a child and instruct him or her not to let anyone see it.

Form a circle and say: **God always keeps his promises and today our Bible story is about God's greatest promise.** Ask:

● **Who can remember what God promised Isaiah?** (That God would send Jesus; that things would be peaceful; that Jesus would be born.)

Say: **That's right! Long ago, God gave that promise to Isaiah to share with God's people. A long time later, God sent the angel Gabriel to tell Mary how she would be part of God's plan to send Jesus to save us.** Hold up the Angel and Mary figures. Ask:

● **What special plan did God have for Mary?** (She would be Jesus' mother.)

Put the figures down and say: **That's right. And God has a plan for all of us. God sent Jesus to save us. Our Bible story today is about how God**

✏️ The Point

kept his promise when ⬤ Jesus came to save us and was born in Bethlehem. God always keeps his promises! I need some volunteers to help me tell today's story. Choose three volunteers and give each one a stick puppet. Explain that they'll hide behind the stage and use their puppets to act

Jesus was born in Bethlehem.

out the story with the *Learning Mat* in the background.

Say: **Now the time was getting very near for Mary to have her special baby. But the king had ordered that all the people in the land go to their hometowns to be counted. That way he'd know how many people were in his kingdom.** Let's see how many children are in our class today. Call up a volunteer to count the children. **Well, that's what the king wanted to do. So Mary and Joseph packed some things on their donkey and traveled to the town of Bethlehem.** Wait for puppeteers to move their figures toward Bethlehem on the *Learning Mat.* **When they got there, it was very crowded. So many people had come to be counted that there was no place for Mary and Joseph to stay! Joseph looked everywhere. Let's help him look.** Have children shade their eyes with their hands and look around the room. **Finally, someone told Joseph that he and Mary could stay in a stable with the animals.** Have puppeteers move their puppets to the stable. Ask:

● **What animals might be in a stable?** (Donkeys; horses; sheep; cows.)

Say: **Let's make the barnyard noises that Joseph and Mary might have heard that night.** Lead children in making animal noises for a few seconds. **Well, right there in that stable, God's Son, Jesus, was born. Now we can bring out our Baby Jesus figure to add to the story!** Have the child holding the figure bring it out and show everyone. **We've been waiting for his arrival!** Instruct the child holding the Baby Jesus figure to tape a soft facial tissue around the figure, like a blanket. **Mary didn't have a crib or a cradle, so she wrapped the baby in cloth and laid him in a manger where animals ate. There's a song that tells about Jesus' birth in a stable. Let's sing "Away in a Manger" together as we pass Baby Jesus around.** Lead children in singing "Away in a Manger" (track 5) with the *CD* while they gently pass the figure around the circle. When the song ends, turn off the CD player.

Sing

Away in a manger, no crib for a bed,
The little Lord Jesus laid down his sweet head.
The stars in the sky looked down where he lay,
The little Lord Jesus asleep on the hay.

Call the puppeteers forward, collect the *Nativity Kit* figures, and put them out of sight. Then ask:

● **What was it like when Jesus was born?** (There were animals; there was no room for Mary and Joseph in a house.)

● **Why wasn't he born in a hospital or a house?** (There weren't any hospitals; it was too crowded; they were staying in a stable.)

● **How do you think Mary and Joseph felt when Jesus was born?** (Happy; excited; glad; tired.)

● **Why is it so important that Jesus was born?** (Because he came to save us; he's God's Son; he's a special baby from heaven.)

Say: **Jesus came to save us and was born in Bethlehem. God kept the promise that he'd made long, long ago. A Savior was born!**

Do the Bible Story (up to 10 minutes)

Say: **Jesus was sure born in a strange place! Our *CD* has some sounds that Mary and Joseph might have heard that night in the stable. I'll play**

● **The Point**

the *CD* and have you guess what those sounds are.

Play the "Bethlehem Barnyard" segment of the *CD*. Pause the *CD* after each noise and allow children to guess what the sounds are. Children will hear cows, sheep, chickens, a donkey, and a hoot owl.

✔ To make this more active, you may want to allow children to act out the animal after they've correctly guessed it.

After the last animal sound, cue the *CD* to track 7 and say: **Let's celebrate Jesus' birth by singing "Baby Jesus" to the tune of "Jesus Loves Me."**

Sing

**Baby Jesus, God's own Son,
Born today in Bethlehem.
Horses, donkeys, cows, and sheep
Watched the little baby sleep.**

He came to save me. *(Point to self.)*
He came to save you. *(Point to someone else.)*
He came to save us. *(Open arms to include others.)*
Because God loves us so! *(Hug self.)*

Say: **Singing is a great way to share good news! Let's share the news about Jesus' birth with our friend, Pockets.**

Practicing the Point

No Kangaroo (up to 5 minutes)

Bring out Pockets the Kangaroo and go through the following puppet script. When you finish the script, take Pockets with you to the Closing. Then put her away and out of sight.

No Kangaroo

PUPPET SCRIPT

Pockets: *(Comes in sadly singing song to "Mary Had a Little Lamb.")* I wish I'd been the little lamb, the little lamb, the little lamb... Oh, hi, everyone.

Teacher: Hi, Pockets! Why are you sounding so sad?

Pockets: We got left out. The sheep were there, the donkey was there—but we weren't.

Teacher: Who wasn't where, Pockets?

(Continued)

Jesus was born in Bethlehem.

Pockets: At the stable! There were NO kangaroos in the stable when baby Jesus was born. I wish a kangaroo had been there, too!

Teacher: Oh, I see. You know, Pockets, just a few animals were there when Jesus was actually born. None of our friends in class were there, either. But we're not left out. God wants everyone to celebrate Jesus' birth.

Pockets: Really?

Teacher: Yes! So you can celebrate right along with the rest of us!

Pockets: Wow! Now I don't feel left out at all.

Teacher: Jesus wasn't born in a fancy place; he was born in a stable. That was God's plan so people everywhere would know that Jesus came for everyone—not just rich people or important people.

Pockets: I'm glad we can all celebrate Jesus' birth!

Teacher: Well, we're getting ready to celebrate Jesus' birth with some special gifts. Would you like to join us?

Pockets: I'd love to! Let's go!

TODAY I LEARNED . . .

We believe that Christian education extends beyond the classroom into the home. Photocopy the "Today I Learned..." handout (p. 56) for this week and send it home with your children. Encourage parents to use the handout to plan meaningful family activities to reinforce this week's topic. Follow up the "Today I Learned..." activities next week by asking children what their families did.

Closing

Hearts for Jesus (up to 5 minutes)

Set out squares of gift wrap, ribbon, scissors, tape, and the hearts children made in Option 1. Gather children and say: ✎ **Jesus came to save us and was born in Bethlehem. God's greatest gift to us is Jesus.** Ask:

● **What is the best gift we can give to God?** (Our love; our hearts.)

Say: **Yes, our best gift to God is our love. Let's gift-wrap the hearts we made earlier as gifts for Jesus. Take them home and put them under your Christmas trees and on Christmas morning you can open your gifts to Jesus and place them on your trees.**

As children work, take Pockets around to talk with children and tell them The Point. After children have wrapped their ornaments, pray: **Dear God, we thank you for giving us the greatest gift of all by sending Jesus to save us. In Jesus' name, amen.**

✎ **The Point**

For Extra Time

If you have a long class time or want to add additional elements to your lesson, try one of the following activities.

LIVELY LEARNING: Baby Jesus

Lead children in singing "Baby Jesus" to the tune of "Jesus Loves Me" without the *CD*. Form pairs and have one partner make up motions to the first verse, while the other partner copies the actions. Then have everyone do the motions for the chorus.

Sing

**Baby Jesus, God's own Son,
Born today in Bethlehem.
Horses, donkeys, cows, and sheep
Watched the little baby sleep.**

He came to save me. *(Point to self.)*
He came to save you. *(Point to someone else.)*
He came to save us. *(Open arms to include others.)*
Because God loves us so! *(Hug self.)*

Sing the song a second time. This time have partners switch roles so each person has a turn making up motions.

MAKE TO TAKE: Bethlehem Journey

Photocopy the "Bethlehem Journey" handout so you have one for each child. Have children cut out the figures and color the handout. Show them how to bend a paper clip and tape it to the Mary and Joseph figures, as shown in margin, then place the figures on the map. Give each child a craft magnet and demonstrate how to hold it under the paper, right behind the paper clip. Children can move the magnet so Mary and Joseph travel to Bethlehem.

TREAT TO EAT: Trail Mix Tally

Set out muffin tins filled with items such as chocolate chips, banana chips, raisins, coconut, or roasted pumpkin seeds. Distribute plastic bags and have children count a certain number of each item into their bags, such as 10 chocolate chips, 15 raisins, or 20 pumpkin seeds. Remind them that Mary and Joseph traveled to Bethlehem because the king counted the people in his kingdom. Explain that trail mix is good to take on a long journey.

STORY PICTURE: Jesus Is Born

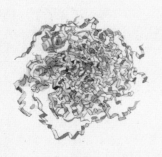

Give each child a photocopy of the "Today I Learned . . ." handout from page 56. Put crayons, glue, and *springfill* on the table for children to use. Invite children to color the picture and then glue *springfill* as hay on the manger and as the floor of the stable.

Jesus was born in Bethlehem.

Bethlehem Journey

Jesus was born in Bethlehem.

TODAY I LEARNED...

The Point ✏ Jesus came to save us and was born in Bethlehem.

LESSON 3

Today your child learned that Jesus came to save us and was born in Bethlehem. Children learned that Jesus is God's greatest gift to us. They discovered that the best gift we can give to God is our love.

Verse to Learn

"A Savior has been born to you; he is Christ the Lord" (Luke 2:11b).

Ask Me...

● Where was Jesus born?
● What is the best gift you can give Jesus?
● How can our family make room for Jesus?

Family Fun

● Make a birthday party for Jesus a key part of your Christmas celebration. Encourage each family member to tell about a gift he or she will give to Jesus in the coming year.
● Go through the Christmas cards you've received. Pray together that the people who sent the cards will know that Jesus came to save them.

Jesus Is Born (Luke 2:1-7)

Permission to photocopy this handout from Group's Hands-On Bible Curriculum™ for Pre-K & K granted for local church use. Copyright © Group Publishing, Inc., P.O. Box 481, Loveland, CO 80539.

Announcing: Jesus' Birthday!

The Point

✎ The angels and the shepherds wanted everyone to know that Jesus came to save us.

The Bible Basis

Luke 2:8-20. The angels tell the shepherds of Jesus' birth.

Would you have been able to keep quiet? The shepherds couldn't! As they quietly tended sheep outside the sleepy town of Bethlehem, an angel suddenly appeared and announced the birth of a Savior whom they'd find lying in a feeding trough! Then the night sky was filled with the glory of heaven as angelic voices praised God. When the angels left, the shepherds rushed to Bethlehem to see this incredible event. And just as the angel had said, there were Mary and Joseph, huddled over a baby wrapped in cloth and lying in a manger. Would you have been able to keep quiet?

Children like to share their knowledge with others. Whether it's a new word they can read, a fact they learned from a teacher, or a family secret; they want everyone to know! What a perfect time to teach them to share the wonderful news of Jesus' birth, just like the angels and shepherds did. Use this lesson to help children understand the excitement of the angels and shepherds and their eagerness to tell others about Jesus' birth.

Getting the Point

✎ **The angels and the shepherds wanted everyone to know that Jesus came to save us.**

It's important to say The Point just as it's written in each activity. Repeating The Point over and over will help the children remember it and apply it to their lives.

Children will
- learn that angels told the shepherds about Jesus' birth,
- discover that the shepherds believed the angels and went to see Jesus,
- celebrate the joy of Jesus' birth, and
- teach Pockets the importance of sharing Jesus' birthday with others.

✎ **The Point**

This Lesson at a Glance

Before the lesson, collect the necessary items for the activities you plan to use. Refer to the Classroom Supplies and Learning Lab Supplies columns to determine what you'll need. Remember to make photocopies of the "Today I Learned…" handout (p. 68) to send home with your children.

Section	Minutes	What Children Will Do	Classroom Supplies	Learning Lab Supplies
Welcome Time	up to 5	**Welcome!**—Receive name tags and be greeted by the teacher.	"Star Name Tags" handouts (p. 30), markers, pins or tape	
Let's Get Started Direct children to one or more of the Let's Get Started activities until everyone arrives.	up to 10	**Option 1: The Confetti Factory**—Make the Shepherds' clothes colorful and make confetti.	Construction paper, glue sticks, hole punch, sealable plastic sandwich bags	Shepherd Nativity Kit figures, angel stamp and ink pad
	up to 10	**Option 2: Green Pastures**—Prepare the Learning Mat pasture for the angels' visit.	Green colored sugar, glue sticks, cotton balls	Learning Mat: Jesus' Birth
	up to 10	**Option 3: Megaphone Mania**—Make angel megaphones to announce Jesus' birth.	"Announcing Angel" handout (p. 67), paper doilies or facial tissue, transparent tape, scissors, crayons, glue	
Pick-Up Song	up to 5	**We Will Pick Up**—Sing a song as they pick up toys and gather for Bible-Story Time.	CD player	CD: "We Will Pick Up" (track 2)
Bible-Story Time	up to 5	**Setting the Stage**—Decorate the room for Jesus' birthday party.	Streamers, balloons, tape	
	up to 5	**Bible Song and Prayer Time**—Sing a song, bring out the Bible, and pray together.	Bible, construction paper, scissors, basket or box, CD player	CD: "God's Book" (track 3), angel stamp and ink pad
	up to 10	**Hear the Bible Story**—Discover from Luke 2:8-20 how the shepherds learned about Jesus' birth.	CD player	Learning Mat: Jesus' Birth, Nativity Kit figures, sticky tak, CD: "A Nighttime Visit" (track 8)
	up to 10	**Do the Bible Story**—Celebrate Jesus' birthday with a party.	CD player, cupcakes, paper towels, frosting, plastic knives, sprinkles, angel megaphones from Option 3	CD: "Baby Jesus" (#2) (track 9)
Practicing the Point	up to 5	**All Year Long**—Teach Pockets that we celebrate Jesus' birth all year long.	Pockets the Kangaroo, bits of tinsel	
Closing	up to 5	**Celebration Share**—Share ways to celebrate Jesus.	Confetti from Option 1	
For Extra Time		For extra-time ideas and supplies, see page 66.		

Jesus came to save us.

Welcome Time

Welcome! (up to 5 minutes)

- Bend down to make eye contact with children as they arrive.
- Greet each child individually with an enthusiastic smile.
- Thank each child for coming to class today.
- As children arrive, ask them about last week's "Today I Learned..." discussion. Use questions such as "How did your family make room for Jesus?" and "What's the most exciting thing about Jesus' birth?"
- Say: **Today we're going to learn that  the angels and the shepherds wanted everyone to know that Jesus came to save us.**
- Hand out the star name tags children made in the first lesson and help them attach the name tags to their clothing. If some of the name tags were damaged or if some of the children weren't in class that week, have them make new name tags using the photocopiable handout on page 30.
- Direct the children to the Let's Get Started activities you've set up.

The Point

Let's Get Started

Set up one or more of the following activities for children to do as they arrive. After you greet each child, invite him or her to choose an activity.

Circulate among the children to offer help as needed and direct children's conversation toward today's lesson. Ask questions such as "How can we celebrate Jesus' birthday all year?" or "What are some things we can do to tell others about Jesus?"

OPTION 1: The Confetti Factory (up to 10 minutes)

Set out construction paper, the *angel stamp and ink pad,* sealable plastic sandwich bags, and the Shepherds from the *Nativity Kit.*

Allow children to make confetti by using hole punches or tearing colorful construction paper into small pieces. Set up an assembly line with some children making the confetti while others put it into plastic bags. Rub a glue stick over the Shepherds' clothing and allow children to sprinkle confetti on top of them to make their clothes colorful. When the Shepherds are completely decorated, set them aside to dry. Tell children that we use confetti to celebrate exciting events. Explain that today they'll hear how the angels and the shepherds wanted everyone to know that Jesus came to save us.

The Point

✔ You'll need a bag of confetti for each child in your class, so have willing children make extras for those who don't choose this Option.

☐ OPTION 2: Green Pastures (up to 10 minutes)

Set out the *Learning Mat: Jesus' Birth,* green colored sugar, glue sticks, and cotton balls. Spread glue over the pasture area of the Learning Mat and allow children to sprinkle the green sugar over it. Then have children glue a few cotton balls on the pasture to represent sheep. As children work, explain that in today's story they'll hear about shepherds who heard a special message in an amazing way!

☐ OPTION 3: Megaphone Mania (up to 10 minutes)

Make several photocopies of the "Announcing Angel" handout (p. 67). Set out the handouts, scissors, facial tissues or paper doilies, crayons, glue, and transparent tape. Allow children to decorate their angels and glue facial tissue or a paper doily to the front. Have them cut along the solid lines for the wings. Show children how to fold back the corners of the paper to make a megaphone. The angel's wings should stand out. Children may use their megaphones during "Do the Bible Story." Tell children that ● the angels and the shepherds wanted everyone to know that Jesus came to save us.

● The Point

When everyone has arrived and you're ready to move on to the Bible-Story Time, encourage the children to finish what they're doing and get ready to clean up.

Pick-Up Song

We Will Pick Up (up to 5 minutes)

Lead children in singing "We Will Pick Up" (track 2) with the *CD* to the tune of "London Bridge." Encourage the children to sing along as they help clean up the room.

If you want to include the names of all the children in your class, sing the song without the *CD* and repeat the naming section. If you choose to use the *CD,* vary the names you use each week.

Sing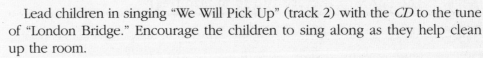

We will pick up all our toys,
All our toys, all our toys.
We will pick up all our toys
And put them all away.

I see (name) picking up,
Picking up, picking up.
I see (name) picking up
And putting toys away.

(Repeat.)

Jesus came to save us.

Bible-Story Time

Setting the Stage (up to 5 minutes)

Tell the children you'll clap your hands to get their attention. Explain that when you clap, children are to stop what they're doing, raise their hands, and focus on you. Encourage children to respond quickly so you'll have time for all the fun activities you've planned.

Say: **Today we're celebrating Jesus' birthday!** Ask:

● **What do you do to celebrate your birthday?** (Have a party; eat cake; sing Happy Birthday; get presents; play games.)

Say: **We'll do some of those things today! We're going to have a birthday party for Jesus! To get ready, let's decorate our room and make it look bright and festive.**

Set out balloons, tape, and streamers and help children decorate the room. When you're finished, say: **We're ready for our party, except for one thing. We haven't sent invitations! But in our Bible story today, we'll learn that God sent the invitations for us because 🖊 the angels and the shepherds wanted everyone to know that Jesus came to save us!**

🖊 The Point

Bible Song and Prayer Time (up to 5 minutes)

Before class, make surprise cards for this activity by cutting construction paper into 2×6-inch slips. Prepare a surprise card for each child plus a few extras for visitors. Fold the cards in half, then stamp the *angel stamp* inside one of the surprise cards. Mark Luke 2:8-20 in the Bible you'll be using.

Have the children sit in a circle. Say: **Now it's time to choose a Bible person to bring me the Bible marked with today's Bible story. As we sing our Bible song, I'll pass out the surprise cards. Don't look inside your card until the song is over.**

Lead children in singing "God's Book" (track 3) with the *CD* to the tune of "Old MacDonald Had a Farm." As you sing, pass out the folded surprise cards. If you want to include the names of all the children in your class, sing the song without the *CD* and repeat the naming section. If you choose to use the *CD*, vary the names you use each week.

Sing

Now it's time to read God's Book
And hear a Bible story.
It's fun to be here with my
  friends
And hear a Bible story.

(Name)'s here.
(Name)'s here.
Here is (name).
Here is (name).
Now it's time to read God's Book
And hear a Bible story.

Now it's time to read God's Book
And hear a Bible story.
It's fun to be here with my
  friends
And hear a Bible story.

(Name)'s here.
(Name)'s here.
Here is (name).
Here is (name).
Now it's time to read God's Book
And hear a Bible story.

After the song, say: **You may look inside your surprise cards. The person who has the angel stamped inside his or her card will be our Bible person for today.**

Identify the Bible person, then have the rest of the children clap for him or her. Ask the Bible person to bring you the Bible. Help the Bible person open the Bible to the marked place and show the children where your story comes from. Then have the Bible person sit down.

Say: (Name) **was our special Bible person today. Each week we'll have only one special Bible person, but each one of you is a special part of our class! Today we're all learning that ● the angels and the shepherds wanted everyone to know that Jesus came to save us.**

Let's say a special prayer now and ask God to help us celebrate Jesus' birthday. I'll pass around this basket. When the basket comes to you, put your surprise card in it and say, "God, thank you that the angels told the shepherds that Jesus came to save us."

Pass around the basket or box. When you've collected everyone's surprise card, set the basket aside and pick up the Bible. Lead children in this prayer: **God, thank you for the Bible and all the stories in it. Teach us today that ● the angels and the shepherds wanted everyone to know that Jesus came to save us. In Jesus' name, amen.**

Hear the Bible Story (up to 10 minutes)

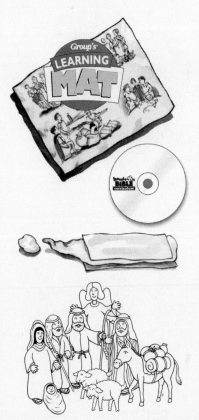

Before this activity, tape the *Learning Mat: Jesus' Birth* to a wall near your story area. Place a small ball of *sticky tak* on the back of each *Nativity Kit* figure, except for the Wise Men and the Camel.

Gather children and say: **Long, long ago God made a promise to Isaiah and all the people.** Ask:

● **What was God's promise?** (Jesus would come to save us; he would send Jesus.)

Say: **God promised that Jesus would come to save us. To review how God kept that promise I'll hold up a figure from our *Nativity Kit*. Then you can tell me everything you remember about that person or thing.**

Hold up the figure of Mary and have children tell you things they've learned about her. Children may say that she's Jesus' mother, God sent an angel to see her, or that Mary went to see her cousin, Elizabeth. Then call up a volunteer and have him or her gently press the figure to the stable on the *Learning Mat*.

Hold up the figure of Joseph and have children tell you what they remember about him. Children may respond that he was a carpenter, that he was Mary's husband, or that he found a stable where they could stay so Jesus could be born. Then call up a volunteer and have him or her gently press the figure to the stable on the *Learning Mat*.

Repeat this process with the Baby Jesus and Donkey figures. Then have volunteers hold up the Shepherd, Sheep, and Angel figures. Say: **On the night Jesus was born, shepherds from Bethlehem were out on a hillside watching their sheep. Then the most wonderful thing happened! I'll turn out the lights so it will seem just like that special night. Let's listen to the Bible story on the *CD* and find out what happened! Listen carefully, so we'll know where to put these shepherds, sheep, and angels on our *Learning Mat*.**

● **The Point**

● **The Point**

Jesus came to save us.

Turn out the lights and play "A Nighttime Visit" (track 8) on the *CD*. Turn on the lights when the angels appear, then turn off the lights when they leave.

When the track ends, turn off the CD player and ask:

● **How do you think the shepherds felt when they saw the angel?** (Afraid; excited.)

● **What did the angel tell the shepherds?** (Jesus had been born; where they could find Jesus.)

● **Where did the shepherds go to find Jesus?** (Bethlehem; a stable.)

● **How do you think the shepherds felt when they saw baby Jesus?** (Happy; excited; thankful.)

Say: **God sent angels to tell the shepherds so we'd know that Jesus came to save all people. ✎ The angels and the shepherds wanted everyone to know that Jesus came to save us. Let's add the shepherds, sheep, and angels to the Nativity scene.** Choose volunteers to gently press the figures to the appropriate places on the *Learning Mat*. Remove all of the figures after class.

● **The Point**

Do The Bible Story (up to 10 minutes)

Before this activity, set out a cupcake on a paper towel for each child, a bowl of frosting, a small dish of colorful sprinkles, and plastic knives for decorating.

Form a circle and say: **Now it's time to celebrate Jesus' birthday! Let's start by decorating cupcakes to enjoy later.** Pass the plain cupcakes, one at a time, to the child on your right and instruct children to continue passing them around the circle until everyone has one. As they pass the cupcakes, have children chant, "Jesus was born on Christmas day. He came to take our sins away!"

When children have finished decorating, gather them together and say: **Let's sing "Happy Birthday" and use our angel megaphones to really celebrate!** Have children use their angel megaphones as they sing, then give three cheers for Jesus. You may want to play a CD of Christmas music as children enjoy their cupcakes. Then gather the children and say: **Now let's sing "Baby Jesus" to the tune of "Jesus Loves Me." Today we'll add an extra verse that tells about the angels and shepherds. It goes like this:**

Shepherds heard the angels sing,
Then went to see the newborn king.
Later wise men worshiped, too
Just like you and I should do!

Say the verse line by line and have the children repeat it after you. Then lead children in singing "Baby Jesus" (#2) (track 9).

Sing 🎼

Baby Jesus, God's own Son,
Born today in Bethlehem.
Horses, donkeys, cows, and sheep
Watched the little baby sleep.

(Chorus)
He came to save me. *(Point to self.)*
He came to save you. *(Point to someone else.)*
He came to save us. *(Open arms to include others.)*
Because God loves us so! *(Hug self.)*

Jesus came to save us.

Shepherds heard the angels sing,
Then went to see the newborn king.
Later wise men worshiped, too
Just like you and I should do!

(Repeat Chorus.)

Say: **Now, let's share Jesus' birthday celebration with our friend, Pockets!**

Practicing the Point

All Year Long (up to 5 minutes)

Before class, drape tinsel around Pockets.

Bring out Pockets the Kangaroo and go through the following puppet script. When you finish the script, put Pockets away and out of sight.

All Year Long
PUPPET SCRIPT

Pockets: Merry Christmas, everyone! Don't you like my Christmas decorations? *(Models tinsel.)*

Teacher: Merry Christmas, Pockets! You're sure wrapped up in holiday happiness!

Pockets: We've been celebrating at home, and I thought I'd decorate myself, too! Christmas is so much fun!

Teacher: Yes, Pockets! We've been celebrating Jesus' birthday, too.

Pockets: *(A little sadly)* I just wish Christmas lasted all year long . . .

Teacher: We CAN celebrate Jesus' birthday all year long!

Pockets: *(Surprised)* We can keep the decorations up and keep giving and getting gifts and eating candy!? That's great! Wait 'til I tell my mom!

Teacher: No, that's not exactly what I meant. You see, Pockets, the most important part of celebrating Jesus' birthday is doing what the angels and the shepherds did.  The angels and the shepherds wanted everyone to know that Jesus came to save us. Children, let's share our Bible story with Pockets. *(Allow children to share about the angels visiting the shepherds.)* Like the angels and the shepherds, we can celebrate Jesus' birthday every day when we share the good news about Jesus' birth.

Pockets: Well, what about the gifts? It won't be much of a celebration without gifts . . .

(Continued)

✏ **The Point**

Jesus came to save us.

Teacher: Oh, Pockets, that's the best part! Each time we share the good news about Jesus' birth we're sharing the best gift of all—Jesus!

Pockets: I like that! A celebration all year long!

Teacher: That's right! We can tell everyone that God's best gift to us is Jesus.

Pockets: Thank you. Goodbye, everyone. Merry Christmas! Happy Birthday, Jesus!

TODAY I LEARNED...

We believe that Christian education extends beyond the classroom into the home. Photocopy the "Today I Learned..." handout (p. 68) for this week and send it home with your children. Encourage parents to use the handout to plan meaningful family activities to reinforce this week's topic. Follow up the "Today I Learned..." activities next week by asking children what their families did.

Closing

Celebration Share (up to 5 minutes)

Gather children and say: 🔹**The angels and the shepherds wanted everyone to know that Jesus came to save us! We can celebrate Jesus' birthday all year long by sharing God's best gift with others!** Distribute the bags of confetti from Option 1. **This celebration confetti is something you can share with others as you tell them about Jesus. Find a partner and sprinkle some of your confetti in his or her bag while you share one thing you love about Jesus.**

After children have shared in pairs, bring everyone together and pray: **Dear God, we thank you for Jesus, your best gift to us. Help us to celebrate Jesus' birthday every day by telling others that Jesus came to save us. In Jesus' name, amen.**

🔹 **The Point**

For Extra Time

If you have a long class time or want to add additional elements to your lesson, try one of the following activities.

LIVELY LEARNING: Celebration Pass

You'll need Life Savers candies (or fruit ring cereal) and plastic coffee stirrers. Form groups of three and within each group have children decide who will be the angel, the shepherd, and the announcer. Give each child a stirrer and each group a Life Saver candy. Say: **Since Jesus came to save us, he's our lifesaver! Let's have a relay to pass on that good news! The angel will put the Life Saver on the stick and carry the Life Saver to the shepherd, who will use the stick to carry and deliver the Life Saver to the announcer. When the announcer receives the Life Saver, he or she will say, "Good news! Jesus came to save us!"** After the activity, throw away the used Life Savers and give each child a clean candy to enjoy.

✏ The Point

MAKE TO TAKE: Angelic Finger Puppets

Gather paper muffin cups, tape, glue, and cotton balls. Give each child two muffin cups and a cotton ball. Demonstrate how to fold a muffin cup in half, then roll it to make a funnel shape. Help tape the edges together. Have children fold their second muffin cups in half and tape them to the back of the funnels to form wings. Demonstrate how to glue the cotton ball to the top of the funnel as the angel's head. As children work, talk about how ✏ the angels and the shepherds wanted everyone to know that Jesus came to save us.

TREAT TO EAT: Peanut Butter People

Before class, mix equal parts of peanut butter and powdered sugar until you have a firm dough. Give each child a lump of dough. Encourage children to use the dough to create something from the Christmas story, such as a shepherd's staff, sheep, a baby, or angels. Talk about the different people that God chose to tell about Jesus' birth. You may choose to let the children eat their dough or place it in sandwich bags to take home.

 ✔ Before preparing the snacks, check to make sure children are not allergic to the ingredients.

STORY PICTURE: Announcing: Jesus' Birthday!

Give each child a photocopy of the "Today I Learned . . ." handout from page 68. Cover a work area with newspapers. Set out crayons, cotton swabs, and glitter glue. Have children color the picture, then spread a thin layer of glitter glue on the angels.

Jesus came to save us.

Announcing Angel

Photocopy the handout. Help children cut along the solid lines, then roll the edges back to form a megaphone.

Jesus came to save us.

TODAY I LEARNED . . .

The Point ✏ The angels and the shepherds wanted everyone to
know that Jesus came to save us.

Today your child learned that the angels and the shepherds wanted everyone to know that Jesus came to save us. Children learned that they can tell others about Jesus, too. They shared ways we can celebrate Jesus' birthday every day.

Verse to Learn

"A Savior has been born to you; he is Christ the Lord" (Luke 2:11b).

Ask Me . . .

● What did the shepherds do when they learned of Jesus' birth?
● How can you share the good news about Jesus?
● What special things can our family do to celebrate Jesus' birth?

Family Fun

● Go caroling as a family (or invite friends to go along) to share the good news of Jesus' birth with neighbors and relatives.
● Use angel-shaped cookie cutters to cut angel-shaped toast for a breakfast treat. Or cut fluffy angels from slices of angel food cake. Decorate them with white frosting and share your angelic treats with elderly neighbors.

Announcing: Jesus' Birthday! (Luke 2:8-20)

The Point

✏ The wise men knew
that Jesus came to save us.

Follow That Star!

The Bible Basis

Matthew 2:1-23. The wise men seek Jesus.

The Bible tells us little about the Magi who came to Bethlehem seeking Jesus. We know they were scholars who studied the stars and other sciences. The costly gifts they carried indicate their wealth. We know they were Gentiles, possibly from Persia, and that they followed a star to find a king. Though we don't know many details about these men, we do know their purpose. They came to worship a king. It didn't matter that the child didn't live in a palace or that his parents weren't wealthy; "they bowed down and worshiped him." The Magi knew the importance of the Christ child, even when God's own people didn't.

Children today don't have to follow a mysterious star to find Jesus. They can learn about Jesus in Sunday school, children's church, a club, and at home. Yet, like the Magi, children need to capture the wonder and excitement in finding and worshiping the newborn King. When we help children discover the joy of worship, we equip them with the tools to grow closer to God. Use this lesson to help children follow the wise men's example of worshiping Jesus.

Getting the Point

✏ **The wise men knew that Jesus came to save us.**

It's important to say The Point just as it's written in each activity. Repeating The Point over and over will help the children remember it and apply it to their lives.

Children will
- discover that God sent the star to lead the wise men to Jesus,
- understand that the wise men came to worship Jesus as king,
- learn that God protected Jesus, and
- help Pockets learn about the best gift to give.

✏ **The Point**

This Lesson at a Glance

Before the lesson, collect the necessary items for the activities you plan to use. Refer to the Classroom Supplies and Learning Lab Supplies columns to determine what you'll need. Remember to make photocopies of the "Today I Learned..." handout (p. 79) to send home with your children.

Section	Minutes	What Children Will Do	Classroom Supplies	Learning Lab Supplies
Welcome Time	up to 5	**Welcome!**—Receive name tags and be greeted by the teacher.	"Star Name Tags" handouts (p. 30), markers, pins or tape	
Let's Get Started Direct children to one or more of the Let's Get Started activities until everyone arrives.	up to 10	**Option 1: Wise Men Munchies**—Decorate tasty wise men as a treat to share.	Gingerbread-men cookie cutters, bread, icing, chocolate chips, gumdrops, red cinnamon candies, plastic knives	Learning Mat: Jesus' Birth
	up to 10	**Option 2: Star Bright**—Make a shiny star for the Learning Mat.	Foil gift wrap, glue sticks	
	up to 10	**Option 3: Camel-Track Trail**—Make camel tracks like the wise men did.	Potatoes, finger paint, bowls, paper grocery sacks, tape, newspapers	
Pick-Up Song	up to 5	**We Will Pick Up**—Sing a song as they pick up toys and gather for Bible-Story Time.	CD player	CD: "We Will Pick Up" (track 2)
Bible-Story Time	up to 5	**Setting the Stage**—Play a "Star Search" game.	Paper stars, tape	
	up to 5	**Bible Song and Prayer Time**—Sing a song, bring out the Bible, and pray together.	Bible, construction paper, scissors, basket or box, CD player	CD: "God's Book" (track 3), angel stamp and ink pad
	up to 15	**Hear the Bible Story**—Help the wise men travel to Jesus and hear of their adventures from Matthew 2:1-23.	CD player, sequins, yarn, glue sticks	Learning Mat: Jesus' Birth, Nativity Kit figures, ring, sticky tak, CD: "We Three Kings" (track 10) and "Wise Men's Worship" (track 11)
	up to 5	**Do the Bible Story**—Sing about the wise men's journey.	CD player	CD: "Baby Jesus" (#2) (track 9)
Practicing the Point	up to 5	**The Best Gift**—Help Pockets learn that the best gift is love.	Pockets the Kangaroo, gift list	
Closing	up to 5	**Jesus Came to Save Us!**—Share cookies and affirmations.	Treats from Option 1	
For Extra Time		For extra-time ideas and supplies, see page 78.		

Jesus came to save us.

Welcome Time

Welcome! (up to 5 minutes)

- Bend down to make eye contact with children as they arrive.
- Greet each child individually with an enthusiastic smile.
- Thank each child for coming to class today.
- As children arrive, ask them about last week's "Today I Learned..." discussion. Use questions such as "How did you tell others about Jesus' birth?" and "What new ways did your family celebrate Jesus' birth?"
- Say: **Today we're going to learn that** ⬤ **the wise men knew that Jesus came to save us.**
- Hand out the star name tags children made in the first lesson and help them attach the name tags to their clothing. If some of the name tags were damaged or if some of the children weren't in class that week, have them make new name tags using the photocopiable handout on page 30.
- Direct the children to the Let's Get Started activities you've set up.

✎ **The Point**

Let's Get Started

Set up one or more of the following activities for children to do as they arrive. After you greet each child, invite him or her to choose an activity.

Circulate among the children to offer help as needed and direct children's conversation toward today's lesson. Ask questions such as "What is God's best gift to us?" or "What gift can we give to God?"

OPTION 1: Wise Men Munchies (up to 10 minutes)

Bring a loaf of bread, gingerbread-men cookie cutters, and an assortment of items such as icing, chocolate chips, raisins, red cinnamon candies, gumdrops, colorful sprinkles, and plastic knives. Let children cut gingerbread-man shapes from the bread, then decorate them with the other items. Have children decorate enough treats for each child to have one during the Closing. Tell children that today's story is about wise men who wanted to find Jesus and worship him. Explain that ⬤ the wise men knew that Jesus came to save us.

✎ **The Point**

OPTION 2: Star Bright (up to 10 minutes)

Lay the *Learning Mat: Jesus' Birth* on the floor or a table where children can reach it. Set out glue sticks and scraps of foil gift wrap. Have children tear the shiny paper and glue bits of it on the large star on the *Learning Mat*. Encourage children to fill in the star completely so it'll look nice and bright for your story today. Explain that today they'll hear about wise men who followed a star to find the baby Jesus.

OPTION 3: Camel-Track Trail (up to 10 minutes)

Have children help you cut several paper grocery sacks apart, then tape them together with the plain sides facing up to form a long "road." Lay this paper road along one wall. Then set out paper plates or bowls of brown or black finger paint and two potatoes cut in half and roughly shaped as camel prints (see illustration in the margin).

Cover a work area with newspapers. Demonstrate how to dip the potato stamp in the paint, then make tracks on the paper road. Explain that today's story is about wise men who rode camels on a long trip to find Jesus. Tell children that they wanted to find Jesus because they knew Jesus came to save us.

When everyone has arrived and you're ready to move on to the Bible-Story Time, encourage the children to finish what they're doing and get ready to clean up.

Pick-Up Song

We Will Pick Up (up to 5 minutes)

Lead children in singing "We Will Pick Up" (track 2) with the *CD* to the tune of "London Bridge." Encourage the children to sing along as they help clean up the room.

If you want to include the names of all the children in your class, sing the song without the *CD* and repeat the naming section. If you choose to use the *CD,* vary the names you use each week.

Sing

We will pick up all our toys,
All our toys, all our toys.
We will pick up all our toys
And put them all away.

I see (name) picking up,
Picking up, picking up.
I see (name) picking up
And putting toys away.

(Repeat.)

Bible-Story Time

Setting the Stage (up to 5 minutes)

Tell the children you'll clap your hands to get their attention. Explain that when you clap your hands, children are to stop what they're doing, raise their hands, and focus on you. Encourage children to respond quickly so you'll have time for all the fun activities you've planned.

Before class, cut stars from yellow construction paper or shiny gift wrap. (You'll need one star for each child in your class.) Hide the stars around the room.

Form a circle and say: **I've hidden some stars around our room. Let's see if you can be good detectives and find them all! When you find a star, bring it back to our circle area and sit quietly.**

When children have found all the stars, ask:

● **How did you know where to look?** (I guessed; I saw one on the wall; I heard someone else find one over there.)

Say: **Today's Bible story is about wise men who wanted to find Jesus. They found a star, too—a special star God put in the sky to help lead them to Jesus.** 🖊 **The wise men knew that Jesus came to save us. We'll hear how their trip to find Jesus was quite an adventure!**

● **The Point**

Bible Song and Prayer Time (up to 5 minutes)

Before class, make surprise cards for this activity by cutting construction paper into 2×6-inch slips. Prepare a surprise card for each child plus a few extras for visitors. Fold the cards in half, then stamp the *angel stamp* inside one of the surprise cards. Mark Matthew 2:1-23 in the Bible you'll be using.

Have the children sit in a circle. Say: **Now it's time to choose a Bible person to bring me the Bible marked with today's Bible story. As we sing our Bible song, I'll pass out the surprise cards. Don't look inside your card until the song is over.**

Lead children in singing "God's Book" (track 3) with the *CD* to the tune of "Old MacDonald Had a Farm." As you sing, pass out the folded surprise cards. If you want to include the names of all the children in your class, sing the song without the *CD* and repeat the naming section. If you choose to use the *CD*, vary the names you use each week.

Sing 🎵

Now it's time to read God's Book	Now it's time to read God's Book
And hear a Bible story.	And hear a Bible story.
It's fun to be here with my friends	It's fun to be here with my friends
And hear a Bible story.	And hear a Bible story.
(Name)'s here.	(Name)'s here.
(Name)'s here.	(Name)'s here.
Here is (name).	Here is (name).
Here is (name).	Here is (name).
Now it's time to read God's Book	Now it's time to read God's Book
And hear a Bible story.	And hear a Bible story.

After the song, say: **You may look inside your surprise cards. The person who has the angel stamped inside his or her card will be our Bible person for today.**

Identify the Bible person, then have the rest of the children clap for him or her. Ask the Bible person to bring you the Bible. Help the Bible person open the Bible to the marked place and show the children where your story comes from. Then have the Bible person sit down.

Say: (Name) **was our special Bible person today. Each week we'll have only one special Bible person, but each one of you is a special part of**

● The Point

● The Point

our class! Today we're all learning that ● the wise men knew that Jesus came to save us.

Let's say a special prayer now and ask God to help us learn how the wise men found Jesus. I'll pass around this basket. When the basket comes to you, put your surprise card in it and say, "God, help us learn how the wise men found Jesus."

Pass around the basket or box. When you've collected everyone's surprise card, set the basket aside and pick up the Bible. Lead children in this prayer: **God, thank you for the Bible and all the stories in it. Teach us today that ● the wise men knew that Jesus came to save us. In Jesus' name, amen.**

Hear the Bible Story (up to 15 minutes)

Before this activity, fold the *Learning Mat: Jesus' Birth* in half, horizontally. Tape it to a wall near your story area so just the starry sky is showing.

Form a circle and spread all of the *Nativity Kit* figures (except the Wise Men and Camel) on the floor in the middle of the circle. Hold up the *ring* and say: **Let's see what you remember about our story. We'll take turns tossing the *ring* into the middle of the circle. Try to make it land on one of the figures, then tell us one thing about the character it lands on.** Pass the *ring* around and have children recall different parts of the story. When everyone has had a turn, put the *ring* away and out of sight.

Say: **You've done a great job of remembering our story! Today's story is about some other people who came to see the baby Jesus. Far away in the east lived men who studied lots of things. They were very smart! One of the things they studied was the stars, and that was how they noticed a new star in the sky. It was a special star they'd never seen before. The wise men knew the star meant that a special child had been born—a child who would be a king. So they got on their camels and followed the star. We can help the wise men follow the star, too.**

Form a line starting at the *Learning Mat* and give each child at least three sequins and a short strand of brown yarn. Stand at the back of the line and use a glue stick to spread glue on the Wise Men and Camel *Nativity Kit* figures. Pass each figure down the line and have children add their sequins to the wise men's robes and their brown yarn to the camel's fur. As children are working, play "We Three Kings" (track 10) on the *CD* and encourage children to sing along.

When the figures reach the *Learning Mat,* have children gather near it. Place a small amount of the *sticky tak* on the back of each figure and allow volunteers to place them on the *Learning Mat.*

Say: **The wise men traveled for a long time and finally reached Jerusalem. There they went to see the King Herod. He wasn't a very nice person and he . . . well, let's listen to what happened when the wise men talked with King Herod.** Play "Wise Men's Worship" (track 11) on the *CD.*

When the track ends, turn off the CD player and ask:

● **Did King Herod really want to worship baby Jesus? Explain.** (No, he was mean; no, he wanted to kill the baby; no, he was lying.)

Say: **You're right! King Herod was a bad guy! Well, the wise men left** and went to Bethlehem. When they found baby Jesus and his mother, Mary, they bowed down and worshiped him. Then they gave him three very special gifts—gold, frankincense, and myrrh. Those were expensive gifts fit for a king! You see,  the wise men knew that Jesus came to save us. Then God warned the wise men in a dream not to go back to King Herod. So they went home a different way and mean King Herod never found out where Jesus was. Ask:

● **Why did the wise men want to find Jesus?** (They knew Jesus came to save us; they wanted to worship him.)

● **How do you think the wise men felt when they saw Jesus?** (Glad; excited; happy.)

● **Why did they bring such special presents to him?** (Because they knew he was important; they knew he was a king.)

Say: ● **The wise men knew that Jesus came to save us. That's why they traveled so far to worship him. And God protected Jesus from King Herod's evil plan. God loves and takes care of you, just like he took care of Jesus.**

● The Point

● The Point

Do the Bible Story (up to 5 minutes)

Hold the Baby Jesus *Nativity Kit* figure. Gather children and say: **Let's sing our Bible story song that goes to the tune of "Jesus Loves Me." I'll pass out the *Nativity Kit* figures to help us with the song. When you hear about the figure you're holding, pass it toward the Baby Jesus figure.** Set the Baby Jesus figure on the floor in front of you. Sing "Baby Jesus" (#2) (track 9) along with the *CD*.

Sing

Baby Jesus, God's own Son,
Born today in Bethlehem.
Horses, donkeys, cows, and sheep
Watched the little baby sleep.

(Chorus)

He came to save me. *(Point to self.)*
He came to save you. *(Point to someone else.)*
He came to save us. *(Open arms to include others.)*
Because God loves us so! *(Hug a friend.)*

Shepherds heard the angels sing,
Then went to see the newborn king.
Later wise men worshiped, too,
Just like you and I should do!

(Repeat Chorus.)

You may want to sing the song again without the *CD* but give the figures to different children. After the song, turn off the CD player and gather together for a group hug. Then say: ● **The wise men knew that Jesus came to save us. They celebrated Jesus' birth by worshiping Jesus and giving Jesus gifts. God wants us to find Jesus, too. That's one reason God gave us the Bible. Let's see if Pockets knows the exciting story about the wise men.**

● The Point

Practicing the Point

The Best Gift (up to 5 minutes)

Before class, make a gift list on a slip of paper. Write several gifts such as a new car, a trip to Disney World, a new set of Legos, or a stuffed animal. Tape the list to Pockets' hand.

Bring out Pockets the Kangaroo and go through the following puppet script. When you finish the script, put Pockets away and out of sight.

The Best Gift

PUPPET SCRIPT

Pockets: Hi, everyone! I'm glad you're here 'cause I sure need some help! *(Waves list.)* I'm trying to figure out what's the best gift for the baby Jesus.

Teacher: Why do you want to give Jesus a gift?

Pockets: Well, after I heard about those wise men giving Jesus fancy gifts, I decided I wanted to give him one, too. I want to show how much I love him, just like they did.

Teacher: So what do you have on your list so far?

Pockets: *(Reads list.)* A new car, a trip to Disney World, new Legos...

Teacher: Wait a minute, Pockets! Those things cost a lot of money for a little kangaroo! Do you think those are the kinds of gifts Jesus wants?

Pockets: Well, I don't know. The problem is I've only got *(looks in pouch)* one, two...two dollars. But I want to give Jesus something really nice to show how much I love him.

Teacher: I've got good news for you, Pockets. The best gift you can give Jesus doesn't cost money.

Pockets: Good gifts ALWAYS cost money!

Teacher: Not really. The gift Jesus really wants is your love.

Pockets: How do I give him that? I can't wrap it up or put a bow on it.

Teacher: Well, can you children think of ways that Pockets can give her love to Jesus? *(Allow children to tell things such as obeying the Bible, praying, and loving others.)*

Pockets: You mean Jesus would rather have our love than anything else? *(Cheerfully)* That's great! Because I DO love Jesus!

Teacher: You know, God gave us the very best Christmas present of all—Jesus!

Pockets: Wow! No wonder Christmas is a time for giving gifts! I'm sure glad you helped me out. I'm going to go home to find new ways to show Jesus I love him. 'Bye everyone!

Jesus came to save us.

TODAY I LEARNED...

We believe that Christian education extends beyond the classroom into the home. Photocopy the "Today I Learned..." handout (p. 79) for this week and send it home with your children. Encourage parents to use the handout to plan meaningful family activities to reinforce this week's topic. Follow up the "Today I Learned..." activities next week by asking children what their families did.

Closing

Jesus Came to Save Us! (up to 5 minutes)

You'll need the treats from Option 1 or another treat.

Say: ✏ **The wise men knew that Jesus came to save us. Let's share these tasty treats together. As we pass them out, find a partner and say, "I'm glad Jesus came to save you!"** Let children pass out the treats and exchange affirmations. Before children eat, pray: **Dear God, we thank you for giving us the best gift ever. You sent Jesus to save us and to teach us about your love. Help us to share the good news about Jesus with everyone we love. In Jesus' name, amen.**

✏ **The Point**

For Extra Time

If you have a long class time or want to add additional elements to your lesson, try one of the following activities:

LIVELY LEARNING: Nativity Kids

Tape the *Learning Mat* to the wall. Have children hold different characters from the *Nativity Kit* and re-enact the Christmas story. If you have more than 13 children, have some students be Herod, Elizabeth, or extra angels.

MAKE TO TAKE: Cardboard Kings

Gather markers, cardboard tubes from paper towels or toilet paper rolls, construction paper or gift wrap, foil, and glue. Cut several 2-inch circles from white, pink, or tan construction paper or gift wrap.

Distribute cardboard tubes. Help children make wise men by covering their tubes with construction paper or gift wrap. Demonstrate how to sculpt a crown from a strip of foil and set it in place. Have children draw faces on the paper circles, then glue them in place.

TREAT TO EAT: Apple Stars

Before this activity, lay an apple on it's rounded side and cut it into several slices. Cut enough apple slices for each child to have two. You'll also need a small jar of cinnamon sugar.

Tell children that they'll be able to find a star in each apple slice. Distribute the apples and see if anyone can find the star in the middle. Help children remove the seeds, then sprinkle the apple slices with the cinnamon-sugar mix. As children eat their apple slices, talk about how the wise men followed the star to find Jesus.

Story Picture: The Wise Men Bring Gifts

Give each child a photocopy of the "Today I Learned..." handout from page 79. Fill the cups of a muffin tin with colored beads and set out glue, scissors, shiny gift wrap, and crayons. Direct children to color the picture and then use the beads to decorate the wise men's clothes. Children may also glue the shiny gift wrap on the star.

TODAY I LEARNED...

The Point ✏ The wise men knew that Jesus came to save us.

LESSON 5

Today your child learned that the wise men knew that Jesus came to save us. Children learned that the wise men followed a star to worship Jesus. They talked about ways they can follow Jesus, too.

Verse to Learn

"A Savior has been born to you; he is Christ the Lord" (Luke 2:11b).

Ask Me...

● How did God lead the wise men to Jesus?
● What gift can I give to Jesus?
● How can our family worship Jesus?

Family Fun

● Make a family Nativity scene by sculpting aluminum foil into different characters involved in the Christmas story. Turn a shoe box on its side and decorate it with raffia and brown paper from grocery bags. Share what it might have felt like to be in the stable the night Jesus was born.

● Share the joy! Surprise an elderly neighbor, church member, or relative by making an old-fashioned popcorn and cranberry garland. Offer to help them put up their lights and decorations.

The Wise Men Bring Gifts (Matthew 2:1-23)

Jesus Grows Up

At Christmas we think of baby Jesus lying in a manger. Then we tend to fast forward to Jesus' baptism and the beginning of his ministry. But what happened between those events? Jesus grew up! The Son of God was a toddler, a boy, a teenager, and then a young man. As Jesus grew, Joseph and Mary modeled a lifestyle of obedience and faithfulness, and provided a healthy environment in which Jesus could grow. Although the Bible tells us little about Jesus growing up, we do know that God's grace was with Jesus in a special way. From his birth, and throughout his ministry, Jesus did what was right.

Children love to imagine what Jesus was like as a child. They may wonder if Jesus really understands their feelings. Did he ever skin his knee? Was Jesus afraid at night? What was his favorite bedtime story? Did he have to eat broccoli, too? Although we may not be able to answer these questions, we can assure children that Jesus was a child and that he experienced the same things most children experience—runny noses, teasing, temptation, and anxious parents. Yet he always chose to do what was right. The lessons in this module will help children see that they can choose to do the right things, too.

Four Lessons on Jesus Grows Up

	Page	Point	Bible Basis
Lesson 6 **Faithful Family**	85	Jesus did what was right and so did his family.	Luke 2:21-40
Lesson 7 **Jesus Obeys His Parents**	99	Jesus did what was right when he was a boy.	Luke 2:41-52
Lesson 8 **When God Smiled**	111	Jesus did what was right and pleased God.	Matthew 3:13-17
Lesson 9 **Tempting Troubles**	123	Jesus did what was right even when it was hard.	Matthew 4:1-11

Time Stretchers

If the ink pad is dry, moisten it with three to five drops of water.

Father, May I? Game

Play this game as you would play Mother, May I? Have children line up along one wall while you stand at the opposite wall. Give a command to each student, such as "David, take three baby steps." The student must then ask, "Father, may I?" or be sent back to the wall. If the child responds correctly, say, "Yes, you may," then have the student follow your instructions to move forward. You may want to give another direction such as, "No, you may not, but you *may* take five giant steps." Again, the child must ask, "Father, may I?" and wait for you to give the OK. As children reach the opposite wall, give each one a stamp on the hand with the *Thumbs Up stamp*.

Explain that Jesus always did what was right and what pleased his heavenly Father. If you have more than 10 children, you may want to call on two or three children at a time. Make the game more challenging by using interesting combinations of hops, jumps, twirl steps, backward steps, leaps, and scissor steps.

Jesus Did It, So Can I!

Use this finger play to help children remember that Jesus did what was right as he grew up.

When Jesus was a little boy (*hold hand low as if measuring*),
His hands and feet were small. (*Hold up hands and stomp feet.*)
He couldn't reach the top shelf (*reach up high*),
For he wasn't very tall. (*Pat top of head.*)
But he always did just what was right (*fold hands in lap*)
From morning 'til day was done. (*Yawn and stretch, then lay head on hands.*)
For Jesus was more than just a boy (*hold hand low as if measuring*);
He was God's own special Son! (*Hug self.*)

And just like Jesus, I am small (*pat head*)
With little hands and feet. (*Hold up hands.*)
It's hard to reach the top shelf (*reach up high*)
And to sit still in my seat. (*Wiggle around.*)
But I'll do my best to do what's right (*fold hands in lap*)
To make my Father smile. (*Point to heaven.*)
For I am more than just a kid (*pat head*);
I'm God's own special child! (*Hug self.*)

Remembering God's Word

Each four- or five-week module focuses on a key Bible verse. The key verse for this module is "Do what is right and good in the Lord's sight" (Deuteronomy 6:18a).

This module's key verse will teach children that doing what is right means obeying God's Word.

The Right Choice

Read the verse aloud and have children repeat it after you. Then say: **God wants us to do things that are good and right. Let's play a game that will help us see what those things are.**

Give sheets of newspaper to children and have them wad their papers into paper balls. Have children sit in a line down the middle of the room. Place a Bible on a chair to the right. Say: **I'll read little stories about different people. Then you can decide whether the people in the stories did what was good and right or whether they did something that was bad. If you think they did the right thing, toss your paper toward the chair with the Bible on it. If you think they did the wrong thing, toss your paper to the other side. Ready?**

Read the following situations, pausing after each one to allow children to "cast their votes." After children have decided, have them retrieve a paper ball (it doesn't have to be their own) and sit down in the line again.

● **Sarah found a $10 bill on the floor at church. She wanted to keep it, but she knew that whoever lost it was probably sad. So Sarah took the $10 bill to the church office.**

● **Andy thought he would play a joke on his mom. When she came to pick him up from Sunday school, he hid behind the bookshelf so she couldn't find him. She was afraid that he was lost.**

● **Kyra brought her new birthday toys to kindergarten to show her friends. At recess, she let everyone except Ashley play with them. She told Ashley that they weren't friends.**

● **Patrick was playing in the living room when he accidentally knocked over his mom's favorite lamp and broke it. When his mom asked who broke the lamp, Patrick told her that he was sorry he'd done it.**

Read the key verse again, then have each child say the verse and toss his or her paper ball into the trash can.

Singin' It Right!

Teach children "Do What the Lord Says" to the tune of "Here We Go 'Round the Mulberry Bush" to help children remember the key verse. This song is not on the *CD*.

> **Do what is right and good,**
> **Right and good,**
> **Right and good.**
> **Do what is right and good.**
> **In the Lord's sight.**

After you sing the song, have children share some of the good and right things that God wants them to do. Children may mention things such as sharing, being kind, helping parents, or being honest. When everyone has shared, sing the song again.

Story Enhancements

Make Bible stories come alive in your classroom by bringing in Bible costumes, setting out sensory items, or creating bulletin boards. When children learn with their five senses as well as with their hearts and minds, lessons come alive and children remember them. Each week bring in one or more items to help involve and motivate children in the Bible lessons they'll be learning. The following ideas will help get you started.

Lesson 6

● Bring in a blossoming plant. Talk about the care and nurture that help a plant grow. Discuss how Mary and Joseph cared for and nurtured baby Jesus so he would grow up to be a healthy child.

● Have a church member bring in a baby and explain what it's like to care for a newborn. Explain that Jesus was just a newborn when Mary and Joseph brought him to Jerusalem. Talk about how important it was for God's Son to have loving and godly parents.

Lesson 7

● Use a roll of shelf paper to make a simple scroll and show it to the children. Allow children to draw pictures of their favorite Bible stories on the scroll. Talk about how in Bible times, scrolls were all handwritten. They didn't have many copies of them, as we have of the Bible today. Explain that people had to memorize the Scriptures and talk about them continuously to remember God's Word.

● Have a pastor come in to answer children's questions about the church. Remind them that Mary and Joseph found Jesus in the Temple, asking the teachers lots of questions.

Lesson 8

● Bring in a jar of honey and pictures of locusts—foods that John the Baptist ate in the wilderness. If possible, bring in a piece of horse hide or some other kind of leather so children can feel what John's clothes might have been like.

● Set out a pie tin of mud, a dishpan of clean water, and several paper towels. Allow children to dip their hands in the mud, then rinse them in the clean water. Explain that John's baptism was a symbol of sins being washed away.

Lesson 9

● Bring in a fresh, fragrant loaf of bread you've baked from frozen bread dough. Pass it around but don't allow children to eat any of it at first. Talk about how delicious this bread would look to someone who hadn't eaten in 40 days. Remind children that even though Jesus was hungry and tired, he did what was right and overcame temptation.

Faithful Family

The Point

✎ Jesus did what was right and so did his family.

The Bible Basis

Luke 2:21-40. Joseph and Mary bring baby Jesus to the Temple.

Parenting is a challenge for any family, but imagine having the responsibility of raising God's own Son! Joseph and Mary had that awesome task and the Bible clearly shows that they made every effort to do it right. When Jesus was still a tiny baby, Mary and Joseph followed the Jewish laws (Exodus 13:2 and Leviticus 12) by taking Jesus to the Temple to present him to the Lord and offer a sacrifice. Because of their obedience, they met a man named Simeon who took Jesus in his arms and thanked God for sending the Savior of the world. Then Anna, a prophetess, praised God for Jesus and told everyone there that Jesus was the promised Savior. God surrounded his Son with those who would do the right things.

Most children get frustrated with their parents' rules and expectations. If children had it their way, ice cream would be the main course at dinner each night, bedtime would be two hours later, and baths would be abolished! It's important for children to understand that their parents' actions are prompted by love and that they're doing what God wants them to do. By looking at Jesus' childhood, children will be challenged to do the right things.

Getting the Point

✎ **Jesus did what was right and so did his family.**

It's important to say The Point just as it's written in each activity. Repeating The Point over and over will help the children remember it and apply it to their lives.

Children will
- learn how Joseph and Mary followed God's law,
- hear what Simeon and Anna said about Jesus,
- help Pockets understand how important families are, and
- thank God for their families.

✎ **The Point**

This Lesson at a Glance

Before the lesson, collect the necessary items for the activities you plan to use. Refer to the Classroom Supplies and Learning Lab Supplies columns to determine what you'll need. Remember to make photocopies of the "Today I Learned..." handout (p. 97) to send home with your children.

Section	Minutes	What Children Will Do	Classroom Supplies	Learning Lab Supplies
Welcome Time	up to 5	**Welcome!**—Receive name tags and be greeted by the teacher.	"Star Name Tags" handouts (p. 30), markers, pins or tape	
Let's Get Started Direct children to one or more of the Let's Get Started activities until everyone arrives.	up to 10	**Option 1: Family Dress-Up**—Pretend to be a family getting ready for church.	Mirror, old jewelry, hats, purses, clothes, scarves, ties, shoes, Bibles	
	up to 10	**Option 2: Family Fans**—Create "fan portraits" of their families.	Crayons, markers, index cards, hole punch, paper fasteners	
	up to 10	**Option 3: Growing Up Healthy**—Plant seeds that will grow throughout the module.	Beans, water, cups, spoons, resealable sandwich bags, paper towels, tape	
Pick-Up Song	up to 5	**We Will Pick Up**—Sing a song as they pick up toys and gather for Bible-Story Time.	CD player	CD: "We Will Pick Up" (track 2)
Bible-Story Time	up to 5	**Setting the Stage**—Surround a trio member with support and obedience.		
	up to 5	**Bible Song and Prayer Time**—Sing a song, bring out the Bible, and pray together.	Bible, construction paper, scissors, basket or box, CD player	CD: "God's Book" (track 3), Thumbs Up stamp and ink pad
	up to 10	**Hear the Bible Story**—Act out the story from Luke 2:21-40 of baby Jesus at the Temple with Simeon and Anna.	CD player	CD: "Simeon's and Anna's Stories" (track 12), Learning Mat: Story Circle 1
	up to 10	**Do the Bible Story**—Care for potato "babies" in an assembly line.	Potatoes, water, bowls, paper towels, soft cloth, baby powder, paper cups, wax paper, rubber bands, fork	
Practicing the Point	up to 5	**Runaway Pockets**—Help Pockets understand how important it is to care for babies.	Pockets the Kangaroo, pencil, sock, bandanna	
Closing	up to 5	**I Love My Family**—Sing a song about young Jesus, then share things they like about their families.	CD player	CD: "Bigger Every Day" (track 13)
For Extra Time		For extra-time ideas and supplies, see page 95.		

Jesus did what was right.

Welcome Time

Welcome! (up to 5 minutes)

- Bend down and make eye contact with children as they arrive.
- Greet each child individually with an enthusiastic smile.
- Thank each child for coming to class today.
- As children arrive, ask them about last week's "Today I Learned..." discussion. Ask questions such as "What was your favorite part of the Christmas story?" and "How did you seek Jesus?"
- Say: **Today we're going to learn that 🔵 Jesus did what was right and so did his family.**
- Hand out the star name tags children made in Lesson 1 and help them attach the name tags to their clothing. If some of the name tags were damaged or if some of the children weren't in class that week, have them make new name tags using the photocopiable patterns on page 30.
- Direct children to the Let's Get Started activities you've set up.

🔵 **The Point**

Let's Get Started

Set up one or more of the following activities for children to do as they arrive. After you greet each child, invite him or her to choose an activity.

Circulate among the children to offer help as needed and direct children's conversation toward today's lesson. Ask questions such as "What do you enjoy doing with your family?" or "How do you think Jesus behaved when he was little?"

☐ Option 1: Family Dress-Up (up to 10 minutes)

Set up a family dress-up center with a mirror, old jewelry, hats, purses, shirts, scarves, ties, shoes, and old suits and dresses. Have children pretend they're a family getting ready for church. Once everyone is dressed, you may want to take a quick trip to the church nursery to see the babies. Talk about how Joseph and Mary took baby Jesus to the Temple, because God's law said to. Tell children that today they'll learn that 🔵 Jesus did what was right and so did his family.

🔵 **The Point**

☐ Option 2: Family Fans (up to 10 minutes)

Set out markers, crayons or colored pencils, and a stack of 4×6 index cards. Have children draw pictures of each member of their families on separate index cards. While children are drawing, explain that in today's story they'll learn about Jesus' family and how they did what was right. Have children use a hole punch to poke a hole at the bottom of each card, then stack the cards together. Help them each attach a paper fastener through the holes to hold the cards together. Show students how to fan out their cards to show each family member, then put them back in a stack as one whole family.

☐ OPTION 3: **Growing Up Healthy (up to 10 minutes)**

Set out resealable sandwich bags, paper towels, plastic spoons, cups of water, and beans. Have each child fold a paper towel and put it in the bottom of a plastic bag, then pour in three or four tablespoons of water so their towels are saturated. Allow each child to sprinkle five or six beans in the bag. Help children seal their bags and tape them to a window. Tell children that seeds need water and sun to grow into bean sprouts. Explain that Jesus needed love and care to help him grow from a boy into a man. Tell children that today's story is about how ⬤ Jesus did what was right and so did his family.

● **The Point**

✔ Use a permanent marker to write each child's name on his or her bag. Each week, encourage children to add a little water to their bags and watch the seeds sprout!

When everyone has arrived and you're ready to move on to the Bible-Story Time, encourage the children to finish what they're doing and get ready to clean up.

Pick-Up Song

We Will Pick Up (up to 5 minutes)

Lead children in singing "We Will Pick Up" (track 2) with the *CD* to the tune of "London Bridge." Encourage children to sing along as they help clean up the room.

If you want to include the names of all the children in your class, sing the song without the *CD* and repeat the naming section. If you choose to use the *CD,* vary the names you use each week.

Sing

We will pick up all our toys,
All our toys, all our toys.
We will pick up all our toys
And put them all away.

I see (name) picking up,
Picking up, picking up.
I see (name) picking up
And putting toys away.

(Repeat.)

Jesus did what was right.

Bible-Story Time

Setting the Stage (up to 5 minutes)

Tell the children you'll clap your hands to get their attention. Explain that when you clap your hands, the children are to stop what they're doing, raise their hands, and focus on you. Encourage children to respond quickly so you'll have time for all the fun activities you've planned.

Form groups of three or four. Say: **Form a circle with your group, then choose one person to stand in the middle of your circle while the others hold hands.** Pause for children to follow your instructions. **I'm going to give some instructions for you to follow. If you're inside a circle, you'll need to go along with whatever your group members do.** Call out the following instructions:

- **take baby steps and touch a wall**
- **tiptoe all the way around the room**
- **raise your hands and shout "Yippee!"**
- **take four giant steps away from me**
- **skip around in your circle**
- **stand up and sit down twice**
- **hop to another group and sing "Row, Row, Row Your Boat"**
- **tickle everyone in your group, then sit down**

Have group members switch roles each time you've given two instructions, so each member has a turn to be in the middle. Then form a circle and ask:

- **What was it like to be in the middle of the circle?** (Fun; crowded; silly.)
- **While you were in the middle, could you have disobeyed my instructions? Explain.** (No, because my friends were doing the right thing; maybe, but it would have been hard.)
- **How did your group help you follow my instructions?** (They pulled me along; they made it fun; they were all around me and helped me do the same thing they did.)

Say: **When you were surrounded by people who were following my instructions, it made it easy for you to follow along, too. God surrounded Jesus with friends and family who would help him do the right things, too. Today we're going to learn that ◗ Jesus did what was right and so did his family. Let's hear how God placed Jesus in a family that would do the right thing and surround him with love.**

◗ The Point

Bible Song and Prayer Time (up to 5 minutes)

Before class, make surprise cards for this activity by cutting construction paper into 2×6-inch slips. Prepare a surprise card for each child, plus a few extras for visitors. Fold the cards in half, then stamp the *Thumbs Up stamp* inside one of the surprise cards. Mark Luke 2:21-40 in the Bible you'll be using.

Have children sit in a circle. Say: **Now it's time to choose a Bible person to bring me the Bible marked with today's Bible story. As we sing our Bible song, I'll pass out the surprise cards. Don't look inside your card until the song is over.**

Lead children in singing "God's Book" (track 3) with the *CD* to the tune of "Old MacDonald Had a Farm." As you sing, pass out the folded surprise cards.

Jesus did what was right.

If you want to include the names of all the children in your class, sing the song without the *CD* and repeat the naming section. If you choose to use the *CD*, vary the names you use each week.

Sing

Now it's time to read God's Book
And hear a Bible story.
It's fun to be here with my
    friends
And hear a Bible story.

(Name)'s here.
(Name)'s here.
Here is (name).
Here is (name).
Now it's time to read God's Book
And hear a Bible story.

Now it's time to read God's Book
And hear a Bible story.
It's fun to be here with my
    friends
And hear a Bible story.

(Name)'s here.
(Name)'s here.
Here is (name).
Here is (name).
Now it's time to read God's Book
And hear a Bible story.

After the song, say: **You may look inside your surprise cards. The person who has the Thumbs Up stamped inside his or her card will be our Bible person for today.**

Identify the Bible person, then have the rest of the children clap for him or her. Ask the Bible person to bring you the Bible. Help the Bible person open the Bible to the marked place and show children where your story comes from. Then have the Bible person sit down.

The Point

Say: (Name) **was our special Bible person today. Each week, we'll have only one special Bible person, but each one of you is a special part of our class! Today we're all learning that ⬤Jesus did what was right and so did his family.**

Let's say a special prayer now and ask God to help us do what is right. I'll pass around this basket. When the basket comes to you, put your surprise card in it and say, "God, please help me and my family do what is right."

Pass around the basket or box. When you've collected everyone's surprise card, set the basket aside and pick up the Bible. Lead children in this prayer: **God, thank you for the Bible and all the stories in it. Teach us today that ⬤Jesus did what was right and so did his family. Amen.**

The Point

Hear the Bible Story (up to 10 minutes)

Before class, cut apart the *Learning Mat: Story Circles,* found in the Learning Lab. Use transparent tape to tape the ends of Circle 1 together. Store the *Story Circles* in the Learning Lab for use in later lessons.

Have children gather around you. Hold up the Bible and say: **Our Bible story comes from the book of Luke in the Bible. As we listen to the story on the *CD*, let's have fun acting it out! I'll need lots of helpers.** Choose volunteers to be Simeon, Anna, Mary, Joseph, and a priest. Instruct the rest of the children to be people at the Temple, walking by or sitting near the action. As children hear the story, encourage them to make motions or facial expressions that go along with their different roles.

Jesus did what was right.

Turn off the CD player and congratulate children on their performance. Form a circle and hold up *Story Circle 1*. Place your fingers on the first 2 dots so the first scene is showing. Say: **Our *Story Circle* shows pictures of the Bible story. Let's see what you can remember. Tell me what's happening in this picture.** (Mary and Joseph are traveling; Mary, Joseph, and Jesus are going to Jerusalem; Jesus' family is taking a trip.) Ask:

● **Why did they have to take this trip?** (To offer sacrifices; because God's law said to; because they were supposed to.)

Turn the *Story Circle* and hold it so the second scene is showing. Have children tell you what's happening in the picture. (The family finally got to Jerusalem; they're closer to the Temple.) Ask:

● **How do you think they felt when they finally got there?** (Happy; nervous; tired.)

● **Why was going to Jerusalem the right thing to do?** (Because it was in God's law; because they were supposed to go.)

Turn the *Story Circle* so children are looking at the third scene. Have children tell you what's happening in the picture. (Simeon is talking to God; Anna is thanking God; Simeon is holding Jesus; Mary, Joseph, and Jesus are at the Temple.) Ask:

● **How do you think Mary and Joseph felt when they heard what Simeon and Anna said about Jesus?** (Good; happy; sad; excited.)

Turn the *Story Circle* and show children the last scene. Have children tell you what's happening in the picture. (The priest is holding Jesus; Mary and Joseph are giving Jesus to God; they're making a sacrifice.) Ask:

● **Why did Mary and Joseph do the right thing?** (Because they loved God; because they followed God's laws; because they loved Jesus.)

Put the *Story Circle* away and out of sight. Then say: 🔵**Jesus did what was right and so did his family. God blessed Mary and Joseph because they followed his laws, and God blessed them by sending Simeon and Anna to tell the people in the Temple good things about Jesus. God wants our families to surround us with love and protection, and to help us do what is right.**

⬤ The Point

Do the Bible Story (up to 10 minutes)

Before this activity, pour a few tablespoons of baby powder or cornstarch into paper cups. You'll need one cup for each group of four children. Cover each cup with wax paper, then secure the wax paper with a rubber band. Use a fork to poke several small holes in the wax paper.

Form groups of four. Say: **Mary and Joseph took good care of Jesus. Now we're going to see what it's like to take care of babies. In your groups, choose a Washer, a Dryer, a Powder Person, and a Bundler.** Pause for children to choose their roles, then hold up a potato. **This is your "baby." It's important to take good care of your baby and handle him or her with gentle care. You'll need to work together to wash, dry, powder, and bundle up your baby.**

Instruct each group to form an assembly line. Give bowls of water to the Washers, paper towels to the Dryers, cups of baby powder to the Powder People, and soft cloths or facial tissues to the Bundlers. On your signal, have groups begin caring for their potato babies by washing, drying, powdering, and bundling them. Remind children that it's not a race and that they need to be gentle with their babies. When each group has finished, collect the babies and ask:

Jesus did what was right.

● **What was it like to care for a potato baby?** (Hard work; fun; busy; I felt silly because it was a potato.)

● **How is that like caring for a real baby? How is it different?** (Both of them took a lot of work; real babies are harder because they can get sick or hungry; it was like a real baby because we had to wash and dry it.)

● **How did Mary and Joseph take care of Jesus?** (They took him to the Temple; they fed him; they helped him grow strong.)

● **How does your family take care of you?** (My mom walks me to school; my dad gives me medicine when I'm sick; they love me.)

◐ The Point

Say: ◐ **Jesus did what was right and so did his family. Your families help take care of you. They want you to do what's right, too. You know, Pockets was here earlier and seemed pretty sad. Maybe we can cheer her up with our story about Jesus' family.**

Practicing the Point

Runaway Pockets (up to 5 minutes)

Before class, bundle up a sock in a bandanna and tie the bandanna to the end of a pencil or a stick. Have Pockets hold this "hobo style" over one shoulder during the script.

Bring out Pockets the Kangaroo and go through the following puppet script. When you finish the script, put Pockets away and out of sight.

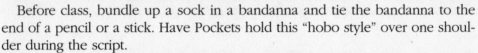

Runaway Pockets

PUPPET SCRIPT

(Pockets enters with hobo pack over one shoulder.)

Teacher: Pockets, what's that you're carrying?

Pockets: *(Sniffling)* It's my clothes and hair bows. I-I'm running away from home and I thought I'd need them.

Teacher: Running away from home!? Why?

Pockets: *(Sniffles turn to anger.)* Well, well, because of my family! They're so unfair...and...and mean, too!

Teacher: Pockets, you have a wonderful, loving family. Why would you ever want to leave them?

Pockets: My parents are always paying more attention to my baby sister. They feed her, give her baths, play with her, hold her...I never get any attention!

Teacher: Your parents love you just as much as your sister. But she's a baby and babies need lots of love and attention. They can't do very much on their own. Even Jesus needed a special family to take care of him. Children, can you tell Pockets what Jesus' family did? *(Allow children to share how Jesus' family did what was right by taking him to the Temple and allowing Anna and Simeon to say good things about him.)*

(Continued)

Jesus did what was right.

Pockets: So you don't think my parents love my sister more than me?

Teacher: Of course not! Remember, you were their little baby once, too. And they took good care of you so you could grow up to be the wonderful kangaroo you are today. They need to give that special attention to your sister, too.

Pockets: *(Thinking)* If I ran away, my parents wouldn't have anyone to help them. Taking care of a baby is a lot of work, you know! Maybe I'd better stick around to help out and show my sister how to be a big kangaroo.

Teacher: That sounds like a super idea.

Pockets: Say, I'd better get back soon! It's almost time for my sister's bath. Mom probably needs me to help out! 'Bye, everyone!

TODAY I LEARNED . . .

We believe that Christian education extends beyond the classroom into the home. Photocopy the "Today I Learned . . ." handout (p. 97) for this week and send it home with your children. Encourage parents to use the handout to plan meaningful family activities to reinforce this week's topic. Follow up the "Today I Learned . . ." activities next week by asking children what their families did.

Closing

I Love My Family (up to 5 minutes)

Say: **Pockets' family would have missed her if she'd run away. They love her so much! I'll bet your families love you all, too. Let's sing a song to help us remember that 🟤 Jesus did what was right and so did his family.**

🟤 **The Point**

Sing "Bigger Every Day" (track 13) to the tune of "Row, Row, Row Your Boat" with the *CD*. Between verses, pause the *CD* and have children share what they like about their families. Children might mention that they like going camping together, that they like getting hugs, or that they like going out for ice cream with their families.

Sing

Grow, grow, growing up *(start in a squatting position, then stand taller on each "grow"),*
Just like Jesus grew. *(Point to heaven.)*
'Though I'm small *(hold hand low, as if measuring)*
I'm growing tall *(move hand higher);*

There's so much I can do! *(Hold hands over head and turn around in a circle.)*
Grow, grow, growing up *(start in a squatting position, then stand taller on each "grow"),*
Bigger every day! *(Reach up.)*
I'll do what's right *(nod head yes)*
With all my might *(flex muscles)*
At church, at home, at play! *(Hop three times.)*

● **The Point**

Say: **When your families do what's right, they're helping you do what's right, too. Let's pray and thank God that ● Jesus did what was right and so did his family.** Pray: **Dear God, thank you for sending Jesus and giving him a special family who loved you and did what was right. Thank you for our families and help us all to do right this week. In Jesus' name, amen.**

Jesus did what was right.

For Extra Time

If you have a long class time or want to add additional elements to your lesson, try one of the following activities.

LIVELY LEARNING: Thankful Cheer

Form a circle and give one student the *ring*. Remind children that Simeon held Jesus and thanked God for sending him. Have children pass the *ring* around the circle while they say, "One and two, three and four, this is what we're thankful for!" The child who's holding the *ring* when the rhyme ends must then share something for which he or she is thankful. Have children continue the rhyming and passing game until everyone has shared a praise.

MAKE TO TAKE: Heirlooms

Make enough photocopies of the "Heirlooms" handout (p. 96) for each child to have one. Set out crayons, pencils, scissors, gift wrap, and other decorative items. Instruct children to color one square on their handouts for each person in their families. Have them draw pictures of things that remind them of each family member, then cut out the heart shapes. Encourage children to put family pictures in the heart shapes when they get home.

NOTE: You may choose to put these "quilt" pieces together to form a wall quilt on a wall of your classroom.

TREAT TO EAT: Graham Cracker Quilts

Set out graham crackers (broken in halves or quarters), softened cream cheese, jelly, raisins, and colored sprinkles. Direct children to make graham cracker quilts by spreading cream cheese on their graham crackers, then adding different toppings to each section. When children put the sections together, they will form an edible quilt. Remind children that babies like to snuggle under warm blankets.

STORY PICTURE: Joseph, Mary, and Jesus in the Temple

Give each child a copy of the "Today I Learned..." handout (p. 97). Have the children color the pictures, then pull cotton balls apart and glue cotton "hair" on Simeon and Anna. Explain that when Jesus' parents took him to the Temple, they were doing the right thing.

Heirlooms

Jesus did what was right.

TODAY I LEARNED . . .

The Point Jesus did what was right and so did his family.

Today your child learned that Jesus did what was right and so did his family. Children heard the wonderful things that Simeon and Anna proclaimed about Jesus. They talked about growing up like Jesus and doing what's right.

Verse to Learn

"Do what is right and good in the Lord's sight" (Deuteronomy 6:18a).

Ask Me . . .

● What were Joseph and Mary doing at the Temple?
● How can you grow up like Jesus?
● What "right things" does our family do?

Family Fun

● Work together to make a batch of muffins. As you work, talk about how following directions are important in making a tasty treat. Explain that God's Word is like a "recipe" for doing what's right.

Joseph, Mary, and Jesus in the Temple (Luke 2:21-40)

Jesus Obeys His Parents

The Point

✏ Jesus did what was right when he was a boy.

The Bible Basis

Luke 2:41-52. Joseph and Mary find Jesus in the Temple.

Joseph and Mary must have been frantic when they realized they'd left 12-year-old Jesus in a busy city, far from home. Since they were traveling with several other families, it would have been easy to assume Jesus was with their group. Returning to Jerusalem, Joseph and Mary anxiously searched for three days before finding Jesus in the Temple. There he sat, surrounded by teachers of the law, listening to them and asking them questions. In spite of his parents' astonishment, Jesus calmly reminded them that this was his Father's house. Where else would he be? He hadn't been disobedient or wrong in spending time there—Jesus was following his Father.

Children may wander off in the grocery store, paint the dog green, decorate the walls with crayon, or flush a toy down the toilet, but they ultimately want to please their parents. Like Mary, Joseph, and Jesus, most parents and children experience times when they seem to be on totally different wavelengths. This lesson will help children learn that Jesus obeyed his heavenly Father as well as his earthly parents. Children will learn that they can do the right thing by obeying their parents.

Getting the Point

✏ **Jesus did what was right when he was a boy.**

It's important to say The Point just as it's written in each activity. Repeating The Point over and over will help the children remember it and apply it to their lives.

Children will
- learn how Jesus obeyed his parents,
- understand how important it is to obey God,
- encourage Pockets to do what is right, and
- discuss ways to obey their parents.

✏ **The Point**

This Lesson at a Glance

Before the lesson, collect the necessary items for the activities you plan to use. Refer to the Classroom Supplies and Learning Lab Supplies columns to determine what you'll need. Remember to make photocopies of the "Today I Learned..." handout (p. 109) to send home with your children.

Section	Minutes	What Children Will Do	Classroom Supplies	Learning Lab Supplies
Welcome Time	up to 5	**Welcome!**—Receive name tags and be greeted by the teacher.	"Star Name Tags" hand-outs (p. 30), markers, pins or tape	
Let's Get Started Direct children to one or more of the Let's Get Started activities until everyone arrives.	up to 10	**Option 1: Ancient Writings**—Write on tablets as students did in Bible times.	Peanut butter, powdered sugar, wax paper, toothpicks	
	up to 10	**Option 2: Play School**—Pretend to be in school.	Blackboard, chalk, paper, pencils, books	
	up to 10	**Option 3: Bean Bogglers**—Play Hide-and-Seek with beans and cups.	Dry beans, paper cups	
Pick-Up Song	up to 5	**We Will Pick Up**—Sing a song as they pick up toys and gather for Bible-Story Time.	CD player	CD: "We Will Pick Up" (track 2)
Bible-Story Time	up to 5	**Setting the Stage**—Search for lost "treasures."	Bible	Learning Mat: Story Circles 1 and 2, egg timer
	up to 5	**Bible Song and Prayer Time**—Sing a song, bring out the Bible, and pray together.	Bible, construction paper, scissors, basket or box, CD player	CD: "God's Book" (track 3), Thumbs Up stamp and ink pad
	up to 10	**Hear the Bible Story**—Meet at the story area, just as Jesus' family met in Jerusalem. Then hear the story from Luke 2:41-52 of Mary and Joseph's frantic search for Jesus.	CD player, yarn, Life Saver candies, masking tape	Learning Mat: Story Circles 1 and 2, ring, CD: "Jerusalem Journey" (track 14)
	up to 10	**Do the Bible Story**—Sing a song and share ways they can do what's right.	CD player	CD: "Bigger Every Day" (track 13)
Practicing the Point	up to 5	**Too Much Fun**—Encourage Pockets to obey her parents and go home from Sunday school, even though she's having fun.	Pockets the Kangaroo	
Closing	up to 5	**Our Father's House**—Share things they enjoy about church, pray and thank God, then enjoy a snack.	"Clay Tablets" from Option 1	
For Extra Time		For extra-time ideas and supplies, see page 108.		

Jesus did what was right.

Welcome Time

Welcome! (up to 5 minutes)

- Bend down and make eye contact with children as they arrive.
- Greet each child individually with an enthusiastic smile.
- Thank each child for coming to class today.
- As children arrive, ask them about last week's "Today I Learned..." discussion. Ask questions such as "How did your family help you do what was right?" and "How did you obey God last week?"
- Say: **Today we're going to learn that 🖊 Jesus did what was right when he was a boy.**
- Hand out the star name tags children made in Lesson 1 and help them attach the name tags to their clothing. If some of the name tags were damaged or if some of the children weren't in class that week, have them make new name tags using the photocopiable patterns on page 30.
- Direct children to the Let's Get Started activities you've set up.

🖊 **The Point**

Let's Get Started

Set up one or more of the following activities for children to do as they arrive. After you greet each child, invite him or her to choose an activity.

Circulate among the children to offer help as needed and direct children's conversation toward today's lesson. Ask questions such as "Why is it important to do what's right?" and "What are some ways you can obey your parents every day?"

☐ OPTION 1: Ancient Writings (up to 10 minutes)

Before this activity, combine peanut butter and powdered sugar until the mixture is dough-like. Give each child ¼ cup of edible modeling dough and a 12×4-inch sheet of wax paper.

Have children fold their wax paper in half, then place the dough between the halves. Show them how to flatten the dough into a smooth "sheet," then lift the top layer of wax paper. Distribute toothpicks and allow children to make letters and designs on their "clay tablets." Explain that when Jesus was a boy, school children didn't have paper so they wrote on clay tablets or in the sand. Tell them that today they'll hear about Jesus going to the Temple to talk to the teachers. Put the tablets on a tray for children to enjoy later.

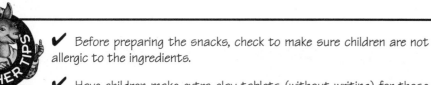

✔ Before preparing the snacks, check to make sure children are not allergic to the ingredients.

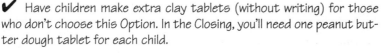

✔ Have children make extra clay tablets (without writing) for those who don't choose this Option. In the Closing, you'll need one peanut butter dough tablet for each child.

Jesus did what was right.

☐ OPTION 2: Play School (up to 10 minutes)

Set up a pretend school center with a blackboard or an easel with newsprint. Set out chalk, paper, pencils, and books and let the children take turns being the teacher. Tell them that in today's story, Jesus amazed the teachers at the Temple with how much he knew about God.

☐ OPTION 3: Bean Bogglers (up to 10 minutes)

At a table, set out three overturned cups and a dry bean. Show children how to place the bean under one of the cups, shuffle the cups, then have another child guess where the bean is hidden. You may want to set up several "Bean Boggler" stations where children can work in pairs. As they search for a hidden bean, explain that today's story is about a time when Jesus' parents searched for Jesus in Jerusalem.

When everyone has arrived and you're ready to move on to the Bible-Story Time, encourage the children to finish what they're doing and get ready to clean up.

Pick-Up Song

We Will Pick Up (up to 5 minutes)

Lead children in singing "We Will Pick Up" (track 2) with the *CD* to the tune of "London Bridge." Encourage children to sing along as they help clean up the room.

If you want to include the names of all the children in your class, sing the song without the *CD* and repeat the naming section. If you choose to use the *CD,* vary the names you use each week.

Sing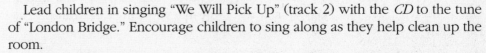

We will pick up all our toys,
All our toys, all our toys.
We will pick up all our toys
And put them all away.

I see (name) picking up,
Picking up, picking up.
I see (name) picking up
And putting toys away.

(Repeat.)

Bible-Story Time

Setting the Stage (up to 5 minutes)

Before class, tape the ends of the *Learning Mat: Story Circle 2* together. Hide a Bible and *Story Circles 1 and 2* in separate places in your classroom. Tell the children you'll clap your hands to get their attention. Explain that

Jesus did what was right.

when you clap, the children are to stop what they're doing, raise their hands, and focus on you. Encourage children to respond quickly so you'll have time for all the fun activities you've planned.

Form three groups. Say: **I've hidden three special things in this room today—two** *Story Circles* **and the Bible. Those are important things since we can't have Bible-Story Time without them! Group 1 needs to find the Bible, Group 2 can find our** *Story Circle* **from last week, and Group 3 will look for the** *Story Circle* **for this week. You'll only have until the** *egg timer* **runs out, so it's important to hurry and find your item. If you see another group's item, don't tell them! Ready? Go!**

Turn over the *egg timer* and encourage children to be careful not to run over each other as they look for their items. As groups find their items, have them sit in a circle. When everyone is seated, ask:

● **What was it like to race the clock as you looked for your item?** (Hard; fun; exciting; speedy.)

Say: **You all did a super job of finding our storytelling tools! Give the person next to you a gentle, friendly pat on the back.** Pause while children follow your directions. **Today we'll hear how Jesus' parents hurried to look for something very important, too. They wouldn't rest until they'd found it! In this story, we'll learn that ✏ Jesus did what was right when he was a boy.**

● **The Point**

Bible Song and Prayer Time (up to 5 minutes)

Before class, make surprise cards for this activity by cutting construction paper into 2×6-inch slips. Prepare a surprise card for each child, plus a few extras for visitors. Fold the cards in half, then stamp the *Thumbs Up stamp* inside one of the surprise cards. Mark Luke 2:41-52 in the Bible you'll be using.

Have children sit in a circle. Say: **Now it's time to choose a Bible person to bring me the Bible marked with today's Bible story. As we sing our Bible song, I'll pass out the surprise cards. Don't look inside your card until the song is over.**

Lead children in singing "God's Book" (track 3) with the *CD* to the tune of "Old MacDonald Had a Farm." As you sing, pass out the folded surprise cards. If you want to include the names of all the children in your class, sing the song without the *CD* and repeat the naming section. If you choose to use the *CD,* vary the names you use each week.

Sing 🎵

Now it's time to read God's Book
And hear a Bible story.
It's fun to be here with my
    friends
And hear a Bible story.

(Name)**'s here.**
(Name)**'s here.**
Here is (name).
Here is (name).
Now it's time to read God's Book
And hear a Bible story.

Now it's time to read God's Book
And hear a Bible story.
It's fun to be here with my
    friends
And hear a Bible story.

(Name)**'s here.**
(Name)**'s here.**
Here is (name).
Here is (name).
Now it's time to read God's Book
And hear a Bible story.

Jesus did what was right.

After the song, say: **You may look inside your surprise cards. The person who has the Thumbs Up stamped inside his or her card will be our Bible person for today.**

Identify the Bible person, then have the rest of the children clap for him or her. Ask the Bible person to bring you the Bible. Help the Bible person open the Bible to the marked place and show children where your story comes from. Then have the Bible person sit down.

Say: **(Name) was our special Bible person today. Each week, we'll have only one special Bible person, but each one of you is a special part of our class! Today we're all learning that ⬤ Jesus did what was right when he was a boy.**

Let's say a special prayer now and ask God to help us do what is right. I'll pass around this basket. When the basket comes to you, put your surprise card in it and say, "God, please help me learn to do what is right."

Pass around the basket or box. When you've collected everyone's surprise card, set the basket aside and pick up the Bible. Lead children in this prayer: **God, thank you for the Bible and all the stories in it. Teach us today that ⬤ Jesus did what was right when he was a boy. Amen.**

✎ The Point

✎ The Point

Hear the Bible Story (up to 10 minutes)

Before this activity, cut 8-foot lengths of yarn. You'll need one length of yarn for each child. Gather the yarn and tape the bunched ends to the floor in your story area. Fan out the other ends and thread a Life Saver candy onto each one. Push the candies about six inches from the free ends and lay them on slips of paper or facial tissues. Leave the yarn and candies fanned out on the floor.

Gather children in a circle in a different area of the room and place *Story Circle 1* in the middle. Say: **Let's see what you remember about last week's story. I'll pass around the *ring* and give each of you a chance to toss it into this *Story Circle*. Then tell us one thing you remember about last week's story.** Give each child a chance to toss the *ring* and share. Then put *Story Circle 1* and the *ring* away.

Say: **In today's story, Jesus has grown up a lot! He's already 12 years old and can do many things for himself. Think about something that you'll be able to do when you're older. Maybe it's staying up later, joining a club, or going to school. When I point to you, tell us one thing you look forward to doing when you get older. Then go sit at the end of a piece of yarn.** Motion to the yarn lengths spread out on the floor. When each child has shared and is seated at the end of a length of yarn, move to the story area.

Say: **There are lots of things you'll get to do in just a few years! Jesus had to wait for those things, too. In our story today, God's people were scattered out, just like you are. Each year in the spring, they'd come together in the big city of Jerusalem for a special holiday called Passover. And when Jesus was 12, he was old enough to go on this special trip. As you listen to the story on the *CD*, slowly move your Life Saver candy toward the story area. Pretend it's a person making the long trip to Jerusalem. When you reach the story area, enjoy your Life Saver candy just like the people in Jerusalem would enjoy a feast.**

Jesus did what was right.

Play "Jerusalem Journey" (track 14) on the *CD*. Encourage children to move slowly toward the story area, then sit quietly, eat their candies, and hear about Mary's adventure. Hold the *Story Circle* so the first scene is showing. Turn the *Story Circle* to show the next scene each time you hear the chime on the *CD*.

When the track ends, turn off the CD player and ask:

● **Why did Jesus' family go to Jerusalem?** (For a holiday; for Passover; for a feast.)

● **Why didn't Mary and Joseph notice that Jesus was missing?** (They thought he was with his friends; there were so many people; they thought he was with the other parent.)

● **Why did Jesus go to the Temple?** (To talk to the teachers; to learn things; to be in God's house.)

Say: **Remember that Jesus was God's Son. When he went to the Temple, he was going to his Father's house. That was a good thing to do! 🖊 Jesus did what was right when he was a boy. He obeyed his Father God, as well as his parents, Mary and Joseph. Let's sing a song about Jesus growing up.**

● **The Point**

Do the Bible Story (up to 10 minutes)

Lead children in singing "Bigger Every Day" (track 13) to the tune of "Row, Row, Row Your Boat" with the *CD*. Play the song once, then pause the *CD* and have children share with a partner one way they can obey God or their parents. Children's responses may include things such as listening to their parents, helping around the house, or doing their chores when they're told to. Then recue the *CD*, play the song again, and have children sing along and do the motions.

Sing 🎵

Grow, grow, growing up *(start in a squatting position, then stand taller on each "grow"),*
Just like Jesus grew. *(Point to heaven.)*
'Though I'm small *(hold hand low, as if measuring)*
I'm growing tall *(move hand higher);*
There's so much I can do! *(Hold hands over head and turn around in a circle.)*

Grow, grow, growing up *(start in a squatting position, then stand taller on each "grow"),*
Bigger every day! *(Reach up.)*
I'll do what's right *(nod head yes)*
With all my might *(flex muscles)*
At church, at home, at play! *(Hop three times.)*

(Repeat.)

Ask:

● **Why is it sometimes hard to obey your parents?** (Because I don't feel like doing what they tell me to; because sometimes other things are more fun.)

● **Why is it important to obey your parents?** (Because I love them; because they love me; it makes God happy; it's the right thing to do.)

● The Point

Say: **As you're growing up, you can try to do right, just like Jesus did! ● Jesus did what was right when he was a boy. Let's see if our friend Pockets is obeying her parents like she wanted to last week. On the count of three, let's call her. Ready? One . . . two . . . three! Pockets!**

Practicing the Point

Too Much Fun (up to 5 minutes)

Bring out Pockets the Kangaroo and go through the following puppet script. When you finish the script, put Pockets away and out of sight.

Too Much Fun
PUPPET SCRIPT

Pockets: (*Looking around suspiciously*) Shhh! Everyone be really quiet!

Teacher: (*Whispering*) Why do we need to be quiet?

Pockets: (*Whispering*) Because I'm hiding from my mommy. I'm having such a good time in Sunday school that I don't want to go home.

Teacher: (*Normal tone*) Well, I'm glad to see you're having such a good time, Pockets. But I think your parents would be worried if they couldn't find you.

Pockets: But I don't want to go home. I want to stay here where we can sing and hear stories and play!

Teacher: This reminds me of our story today. Children, can you share with Pockets about the adventure that Mary and Joseph had?

(*Let a few children briefly tell the story of Jesus remaining in Jerusalem at the Temple. Be sure children include the fact that Mary and Joseph were worried.*)

Pockets: Wow, so Jesus was having such a good time that he didn't want to go home?

Teacher: Well, not exactly. Jesus stayed in Jerusalem to talk with the teachers in the Temple about God's Word. And do you know what Jesus did when his parents came to get him?

Pockets: (*Pauses, thinking*) He went home with them.

Teacher: You're right, he obeyed his parents and went home.

● The Point

Pockets: ● Jesus did what was right when he was a boy. I want to do right, too. So I'd better let my parents know I'm ready to go home. (*Cheerfully*) At least I know I can come back next week and have fun all over again!

(*Continued*)

Jesus did what was right.

Teacher: That's a great attitude, Pockets. We'll look forward to seeing you then!

Pockets: 'Bye, everyone! Be sure to visit me next week!

TODAY I LEARNED...

We believe that Christian education extends beyond the classroom into the home. Photocopy the "Today I Learned..." handout (p. 109) for this week and send it home with your children. Encourage parents to use the handout to plan meaningful family activities to reinforce this week's topic. Follow up the "Today I Learned..." activities next week by asking children what their families did.

Closing

Our Father's House (up to 5 minutes)

Distribute the modeling dough clay tablets from Option 1.

Say: **God is Jesus' Father. Jesus went to the Temple to spend time in his Father's house. When you come to church, you're spending time in God's house, too! On your tablet, draw a picture of something that you enjoy about coming to church. Or you may choose to use your edible dough to make a sculpture of something you enjoy at church.**

Allow children to work for a moment, then have them tell a partner about what they drew or sculpted. Pray: **Dear God, thank you that we can come to your house each week and learn about you. And thank you for teaching us that Jesus did what was right when he was a boy. Help us to be like Jesus and do what's right as we grow up. Thank you for loving us and being our Heavenly Father. In Jesus' name, amen.**

Let children eat their snacks.

● The Point

For Extra Time

If you have a long class time or want to add additional elements to your lesson, try one of the following activities.

LIVELY LEARNING: Jerusalem Jaunt

Before this activity, hide paper hearts at one end of the room. You'll need one heart for each child.

Have children form a line at the opposite end of the room. Tell them that just as Mary and Joseph hurried back to Jerusalem to look for Jesus, they must hurry to look for paper hearts. Tap the first person in line and say "go." Direct him or her to take giant steps to the other side of the room, find a paper heart, bring it back, and tag the next person in line. Continue until each person has found a heart. Then hide the hearts and play again. Remind children that Mary and Joseph were anxious to find Jesus in the crowded city of Jerusalem.

MAKE TO TAKE: Roll a Scroll

Set out crayons or markers and 2-foot sections of shelf paper. Encourage children to draw pictures of their favorite Bible stories or characters on the paper. When they've finished drawing, help children roll their shelf paper from both edges to form a scroll. Show children how to tie their scrolls with lengths of ribbon or yarn. Remind children that when Jesus was a boy, the Bible wasn't a book, but a scroll. Explain that the teachers Jesus talked with knew the Bible very well.

TREAT TO EAT: Tasty Temple Steps

Before class, cut an angel food cake into 1-inch cubes. Give each child some cake cubes on a paper plate and let children build Temple steps with the cake. Explain that Jesus was sitting on the Temple steps with the teachers of the law when his parents found him. Children may want to have several strawberries "sit" on the steps before eating the tasty treat!

STORY PICTURE: Jesus in the Temple

Give each child a copy of the "Today I Learned..." handout (p. 109). Place glue, crayons, and bowls of salt on the table. Direct children to color their handouts. Then have the children spread glue on the steps of the Temple and sprinkle salt over them so they shine like sparkly stones. Explain that when Jesus' parents found him, he obeyed them and went home.

TODAY I LEARNED...

The Point ● Jesus did what was right when he was a boy.

Today your child learned that Jesus did what was right when he was a boy. Children discovered that Jesus talked with teachers and amazed them with how much he knew about God. They talked about ways that they can obey and do what's right.

Verse to Learn

"Do what is right and good in the Lord's sight" (Deuteronomy 6:18a).

Ask Me...

● Why did Jesus go to the Temple?
● Why is it important to obey your parents?
● How can we help each other do what's right?

Family Fun

● Have family members make paper chains for each other to illustrate times they do what's right. Each time a family member catches someone else doing something good, have him or her add a link to that person's paper chain. Family members may add links for things such as brushing teeth, playing cooperatively, saying kind words, sharing toys, giving hugs, cleaning up, eating meals without complaining, and helping others. Hang the paper chains in a prominent place and encourage everyone to make their chains grow!

Jesus in the Temple (Luke 2:41-52)

LESSON 8

When God Smiled

The Bible Basis

Matthew 3:13-17. Jesus is baptized by John.

John the Baptist embraced a simple existence, living on locusts and wild honey in the Judean desert. In addition to setting an example of self-denial, John preached a compelling message of repentance, urging people to turn away from sin and prepare for the coming of the kingdom of God. When people listened and confessed their sins, John baptized them in the waters of the Jordan River. When Jesus came to be baptized, John was troubled. "You, Lord? If anything, you should be baptizing me!" God's perfect Son certainly didn't need to repent, yet Jesus insisted, knowing that it was what God wanted. As Jesus came up out of the water, the Spirit descended on him like a dove, and a voice from heaven said, "This is my Son, whom I love, and I am very pleased with him."

Jesus' willingness to be baptized sprang from a desire to please God. We often see that same trait in children. They love knowing they've pleased someone, particularly a parent or teacher. They'll often go out of their way to let you know that they've followed instructions and obeyed, to receive a word of encouragement, a smile, or a hug. Use this lesson to help children realize that they can please God by doing what is right.

Getting the Point

✏ **Jesus did what was right and pleased God.**

It's important to say The Point just as it's written in each activity. Repeating The Point over and over will help the children remember it and apply it to their lives.

Children will

● hear a story about Jesus' baptism,
● learn how Jesus pleased God,
● help Pockets please her mother, and
● think of ways they can please God.

✏ **The Point**

This Lesson at a Glance

Before the lesson, collect the necessary items for the activities you plan to use. Refer to the Classroom Supplies and Learning Lab Supplies columns to determine what you'll need. Remember to make photocopies of the "Today I Learned…" handout (p. 121) to send home with your children.

Section	Minutes	What Children Will Do	Classroom Supplies	Learning Lab Supplies
Welcome Time	up to 5	**Welcome!**—Receive name tags and be greeted by the teacher.	"Star Name Tags" handouts (p. 30), markers, pins or tape	
Let's Get Started Direct children to one or more of the Let's Get Started activities until everyone arrives.	up to 10	**Option 1: Clean Coins**—Wash pennies in a vinegar and salt solution.	Bowls, vinegar, salt, dirty pennies, soft cloths	
	up to 10	**Option 2: Fine Feathers**—Make dove feathers to use during "Hear the Bible Story."	White paper, scissors	
	up to 10	**Option 3: Sandy "Desserts"**—Help prepare a "sandy" snack.	Graham crackers, instant pudding mix, milk, a bowl, plastic spoons, paper cups, paper plates	
Pick-Up Song	up to 5	**We Will Pick Up**—Sing a song as they pick up toys and gather for Bible-Story Time.	CD player	CD: "We Will Pick Up" (track 2)
Bible-Story Time	up to 5	**Setting the Stage**—Follow fun instructions as they listen for a cue to turn around.	Empty 2-liter soda container, dry beans	
	up to 5	**Bible Song and Prayer Time**—Sing a song, bring out the Bible, and pray together.	Bible, construction paper, scissors, basket or box, CD player	CD: "God's Book" (track 3), Thumbs Up stamp and ink pad
	up to 10	**Hear the Bible Story**—Hold up their Fine Feathers when they hear Jesus doing right in the story of Jesus' baptism from Matthew 3:3-17.	CD player, Fine Feathers from Option 2	Learning Mat: Story Circle 3, CD: "At the Jordan River" (track 15) and "I Love Jesus" (track 16)
	up to 10	**Do the Bible Story**—Share things they can do to please God.		
Practicing the Point	up to 5	**Pockets Pleases**—Help Pockets find something to do that would please her mother.	Pockets the Kangaroo, a Fine Feather from Option 2	
Closing	up to 5	**Sandy Snacks**—Thank God for loving them, then enjoy a snack.	Snacks from Option 3, plastic spoons	
For Extra Time		For extra-time ideas and supplies, see page 120.		

Jesus did what was right.

Welcome Time

Welcome! (up to 5 minutes)

- Bend down and make eye contact with children as they arrive.
- Greet each child individually with an enthusiastic smile.
- Thank each child for coming to class today.
- As children arrive, ask them about last week's "Today I Learned..." discussion. Ask questions such as "How did you obey your parents?" and "How did it feel to do the right things?"
- Say: **Today we're going to learn that ● Jesus did what was right and pleased God.**
- Hand out the star name tags children made in Lesson 1 and help them attach the name tags to their clothing. If some of the name tags were damaged or if some of the children weren't in class that week, have them make new name tags using the photocopiable patterns on page 30.
- Direct children to the Let's Get Started activities you've set up.

● The Point

Let's Get Started

Set up one or more of the following activities for children to do as they arrive. After you greet each child, invite him or her to choose an activity.

Circulate among the children to offer help as needed and direct children's conversation toward today's lesson. Ask questions such as "How do you feel when you're all clean?" or "Have you ever seen anyone get baptized?"

☐ Option 1: Clean Coins (up to 10 minutes)

Before class, combine one-quarter cup vinegar and one-half teaspoon salt in a small bowl. Set out three or four bowls of the salt-vinegar mixture, soft cloths, and a jar of dirty pennies.

Have each child drop a penny into the salt-vinegar mixture. After a few seconds, let them fish the pennies out and rub the pennies with a soft cloth. Point out how shiny the pennies have become! Tell children that today they'll hear about a man who baptized people. Explain that baptism shows others that God has washed the bad things out of our lives and that we don't want to do those bad things anymore.

☐ Option 2: Fine Feathers (up to 10 minutes)

Before class, use the stencil pattern on this page to outline several feathers on white paper. Have the children cut out the feather shapes. Then show them how to cut slits along both sides of their feathers. Allow children to make extra feathers for others to use during "Hear the Bible Story." Explain that they'll hear about a time when God's Spirit came down on Jesus like a dove.

Jesus did what was right.

OPTION 3: Sandy "Desserts" (up to 10 minutes)

Place paper plates, plastic spoons, paper cups, and graham crackers on a table. Form two groups—the Sand Makers and the Soil Makers. Give two graham crackers to each Sand Maker and direct them to rub the crackers together to form graham cracker "sand" on a paper plate. Have the Soil Makers help you stir 2 cups of milk into a bowl with a package of instant pudding mix. Have them stir until the pudding starts to become thick. Then allow the Soil Makers to help you spoon the pudding into paper cups and have the Sand Makers sprinkle the graham cracker sand over the top. Tell children that someone in today's story lived in a sandy desert area. Explain that they'll learn that ● Jesus did what was right and pleased God.

● The Point

Have a helper put the sandy desserts in a refrigerator until the Closing.

When everyone has arrived and you're ready to move on to the Bible-Story Time, encourage the children to finish what they're doing and get ready to clean up.

Pick-Up Song

We Will Pick Up (up to 5 minutes)

Lead children in singing "We Will Pick Up" (track 2) with the *CD* to the tune of "London Bridge." Encourage children to sing along as they help clean up the room.

If you want to include the names of all the children in your class, sing the song without the *CD* and repeat the naming section. If you choose to use the *CD*, vary the names you use each week.

Sing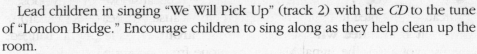

We will pick up all our toys,
All our toys, all our toys.
We will pick up all our toys
And put them all away.

I see (name) picking up,
Picking up, picking up.
I see (name) picking up
And putting toys away.

(Repeat.)

Bible-Story Time

Setting the Stage (up to 5 minutes)

Before this activity, pour one-half cup of dry beans into a clean, empty 2-liter soda container and tighten the lid.

Tell the children you'll clap your hands to get their attention. Explain that when you clap, the children are to stop what they're doing, raise their hands,

Jesus did what was right.

and focus on you. Encourage children to respond quickly so you'll have time for all the fun activities you've planned.

Have children stand in a large circle facing away from the center. Choose a volunteer to be the Signal Master. Give the Signal Master the 2-liter container and have him or her stand in the middle of the circle.

Say: **I'm going to call out some fun instructions for you to follow. While you're doing these silly things, the Signal Master will shake the signal. When you hear the signal, stop what you're doing and turn around as fast as you can, face the center, and freeze. The first person to turn around and freeze will become the next Signal Master. We'll play until several people have had a chance to be the Signal Master.**

Call out the following directions. Allow children to enjoy each task before calling out the next one. The Signal Master may shake the signal any time during the game. You may want to add some fun instructions of your own.

- **Sing "Happy Birthday" to your shoes.**
- **Stand on one foot and flap your arms.**
- **Make animal noises.**
- **Hop up and down saying, "Boing, boing, boing."**
- **Pretend the wall is a mirror and you're fixing your hair.**
- **Juggle imaginary watermelons.**
- **Make a face like you've just eaten pickle pizza.**

Play until several children have had a turn to be the Signal Master. Repeat the above instructions if necessary. Then put the signal away and have children sit down. Ask:

- **Why did you turn around in this game?** (Because we were supposed to; because I wanted to be the Signal Master; because we heard the signal.)
- **What happened when we all turned around?** (The game changed; someone got to be the Signal Master; everyone froze in place.)

Say: **Most of you wanted to turn away from our silly actions so you'd get to use the signal. Today we're going to hear about a man named John who spent his whole life trying to get people to turn away from the bad things they were doing and start living for God. John's work was so important that even Jesus came to him. We'll learn that ◐ Jesus did what was right and pleased God.**

◐ The Point

Bible Song and Prayer Time (up to 5 minutes)

Before class, make surprise cards for this activity by cutting construction paper into 2×6-inch slips. Prepare a surprise card for each child, plus a few extras for visitors. Fold the cards in half, then stamp the *Thumbs Up stamp* inside one of the surprise cards. Mark Matthew 3:13-17 in the Bible you'll be using.

Have children sit in a circle. Say: **Now it's time to choose a Bible person to bring me the Bible marked with today's Bible story. As we sing our Bible song, I'll pass out the surprise cards. Don't look inside your surprise card until the song is over.**

Lead children in singing "God's Book" (track 3) with the *CD* to the tune of "Old MacDonald Had a Farm." As you sing, pass out the folded surprise cards. If you want to include the names of all the children in your class, sing the song without the *CD* and repeat the naming section. If you choose to use the *CD*, vary the names you use each week.

Sing

Now it's time to read God's Book
And hear a Bible story.
It's fun to be here with my
    friends
And hear a Bible story.
	Now it's time to read God's Book
	And hear a Bible story.
	It's fun to be here with my
	    friends
	And hear a Bible story.

(Name)'s here. (Name)'s here. Here is (name). Here is (name). Now it's time to read God's Book And hear a Bible story.	(Name)'s here. (Name)'s here. Here is (name). Here is (name). Now it's time to read God's Book And hear a Bible story.

After the song, say: **You may look inside your surprise cards. The person who has the Thumbs Up stamped inside his or her card will be our Bible person for today.**

Identify the Bible person, then have the rest of the children clap for him or her. Ask the Bible person to bring you the Bible. Help the Bible person open the Bible to the marked place and show children where your story comes from. Then have the Bible person sit down.

Say: (Name) **was our special Bible person today. Each week, we'll have only one special Bible person, but each one of you is a special part of our class! Today we're all learning that** ⚫ **Jesus did what was right and pleased God.**

Let's say a special prayer now and ask God to help us do what is right and please him. I'll pass around this basket. When the basket comes to you, put your surprise card in it and say, "God, please help me do what is right and please you."

Pass around the basket or box. When you've collected everyone's surprise card, set the basket aside and pick up the Bible. Lead children in this prayer: **God, thank you for the Bible and all the stories in it. Teach us today that** ⚫ **Jesus did what was right and pleased you. Amen.**

⚫ **The Point**

⚫ **The Point**

Hear the Bible Story (up to 10 minutes)

Bring out the *Learning Mat: Story Circle 3.* Have children gather around you. Say: **Our Bible story comes from the book of Matthew in the Bible. Our** *Story Circle* **shows us pictures of our Bible story.**

Give each child one of the Fine Feathers from Option 2. Say: **Every time you hear the name "Jesus" on the** *CD,* **wave your feathers over your heads. Listen carefully!** Play "At the Jordan River" (track 15) on the *CD.* Each time you hear the chime, turn the circle so children can see the next part of the story.

When the track ends, have children put their feathers aside. Ask:
● **Why did people get baptized?** (To show that their sins were washed away; to show that they wanted to change.)

● **Why was John surprised that Jesus wanted to be baptized?** (Because he didn't have any sins; he'd always done what was right; Jesus was so good.)

● **What did the voice from heaven say?** (That Jesus was God's Son; that God was pleased with Jesus; that God loved Jesus.)

Jesus did what was right.

● **How do you think Jesus felt after hearing God's message to him?** (Happy; loved; good).

Say: **We've been learning a lot about Jesus doing right. Let's sing a song that will help us remember to do what's right, too.**

Lead children in singing "I Love Jesus" (track 16) to the tune of "London Bridge" with the *CD*.

Sing

Jesus did just what was right,
Every day,
Every night.
He was pleasing in God's sight.
I love Jesus!

I can try to do what's right,
Every day,
Every night.
I'll be pleasing in God's sight—
I love Jesus!

Say: 🖊 **Jesus did what was right and pleased God. God wants us to please him, too. We'll hear lots of ways to do that in our next activity!**

🖊 **The Point**

Do the Bible Story (up to 10 minutes)

Have children form two circles, one inside the other, with the same number of children in each circle. Say: 🖊 **Jesus did what was right and pleased God. When we do things that are right, we please God, too. This action rhyme will help you think of things you can do to please God.**

🖊 **The Point**

Lead children in the following action rhyme. Direct the children in each circle to move in opposite directions as they say the rhyme.

Hop, hop. *(Hop twice.)*
Step, step. *(Step twice.)*
Jump—one, two! *(Jump twice.)*
Jesus wanted to please God. *(Clap on each word.)*
And I do, too! *(Point to self.)*

Instruct children to stop on the last phrase, then pair up with the closest person in the other circle. Have each partner share one thing he or she can do to please God. Children may say things such as obeying parents, helping around the house, praying, singing Bible songs, or being kind to their friends. Repeat the rhyme several times so children have a chance to think of and hear lots of ways to please God.

After the last repetition, have partners sit together and discuss these questions:

● **Why is it important to please God?** (To show that we love him; because God wants what's best for us; because we're his followers.)

● **What's one way you'll please God this week?** (I'll be nice to my little brother; I'll share my toys at school; I'll sing Bible songs.)

Say: 🖊 **Jesus did what was right and pleased God. You've all thought of lots of ways that you can please God. Take your feathers home as a reminder to do what's right and to please God. I made an extra feather for our friend Pockets. Let's call her out and I'll give it to her. Pockets! Pockets!**

🖊 **The Point**

Practicing the Point

Pockets Pleases (up to 5 minutes)

Before this activity, make a Fine Feather from Option 2 for Pockets and bring it to the story area.

Bring out Pockets the Kangaroo and go through the following puppet script. When you finish the script, put Pockets away and out of sight.

 **The Point**

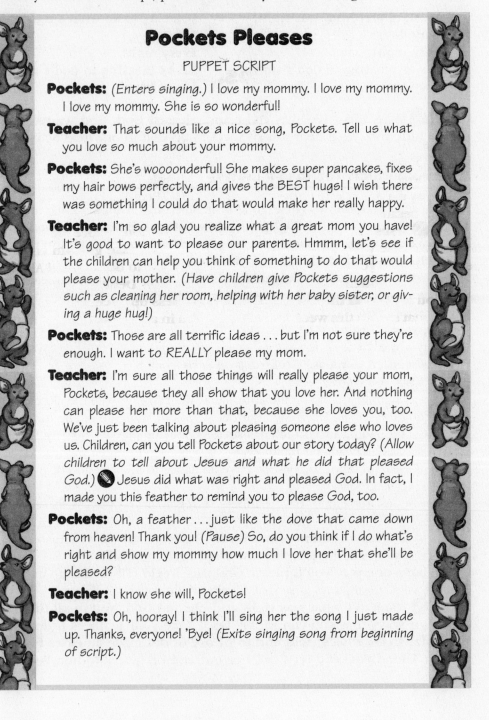

Pockets Pleases

PUPPET SCRIPT

Pockets: *(Enters singing.)* I love my mommy. I love my mommy. I love my mommy. She is so wonderful!

Teacher: That sounds like a nice song, Pockets. Tell us what you love so much about your mommy.

Pockets: She's wooooonderful! She makes super pancakes, fixes my hair bows perfectly, and gives the BEST hugs! I wish there was something I could do that would make her really happy.

Teacher: I'm so glad you realize what a great mom you have! It's good to want to please our parents. Hmmm, let's see if the children can help you think of something to do that would please your mother. *(Have children give Pockets suggestions such as cleaning her room, helping with her baby sister, or giving a huge hug!)*

Pockets: Those are all terrific ideas . . . but I'm not sure they're enough. I want to REALLY please my mom.

Teacher: I'm sure all those things will really please your mom, Pockets, because they all show that you love her. And nothing can please her more than that, because she loves you, too. We've just been talking about pleasing someone else who loves us. Children, can you tell Pockets about our story today? *(Allow children to tell about Jesus and what he did that pleased God.)* Jesus did what was right and pleased God. In fact, I made you this feather to remind you to please God, too.

Pockets: Oh, a feather . . . just like the dove that came down from heaven! Thank you! *(Pause)* So, do you think if I do what's right and show my mommy how much I love her that she'll be pleased?

Teacher: I know she will, Pockets!

Pockets: Oh, hooray! I think I'll sing her the song I just made up. Thanks, everyone! 'Bye! *(Exits singing song from beginning of script.)*

Jesus did what was right.

TODAY I LEARNED...

We believe that Christian education extends beyond the classroom into the home. Photocopy the "Today I Learned..." handout (p. 121) for this week and send it home with your children. Encourage parents to use the handout to plan meaningful family activities to reinforce this week's topic. Follow up the "Today I Learned..." activities next week by asking children what their families did.

Closing

Sandy Snacks (up to 5 minutes)

Have children sit at tables while you distribute the "sandy desserts" from Option 3. Ask:

● **Who lived in the desert and baptized people in the river?** (John.)

● **Why did Jesus want John to baptize him?** (Because that was what God wanted; because it was the right thing to do.)

Say: ●**Jesus did what was right and pleased God. Before we eat our "deserts," use your finger to make a path through the graham cracker sand. Pretend you're making a path that will lead to doing right!** Allow a moment for children to make their paths. Then pray: **Dear God, thank you that you love us all the time, even when we mess up. Help us do our best to do what's right this week and to please you in all we do. In Jesus' name, amen.**

● **The Point**

Jesus did what was right.

For Extra Time

If you have a long class time or want to add additional elements to your lesson, try one of the following activities.

LIVELY LEARNING: Hop, Step, and Jump Charades

Form pairs and have partners link arms as they do the following action rhyme.

Hop, hop. *(Hop twice.)*
Step, step. *(Step twice.)*
Jump—one, two! *(Jump twice.)*
Jesus wanted to please God. *(Clap on each word.)*
And I do, too! *(Point to self.)*

At the end of the verse, choose a pair to act out something that would be pleasing to God, such as giving a gentle hug, helping push in chairs or cleaning up, saying kind and encouraging words, or singing a Bible song. Then repeat the rhyme and choose another pair to show pleasing actions.

MAKE TO TAKE: Delightful Doves

Before this activity, trace the dove figure shown on this page. You'll need a dove figure for each child. Have the children cut out their dove shapes, then punch two holes in their doves, one near the top in the middle and one just below it. Demonstrate how to thread two 4-inch lengths of white ribbon through the lower hole to form wings. Provide an 8-inch length of colored ribbon to loop through the upper hole and tie to make a hanger. As children are working, discuss how God's Spirit came down on Jesus in the form of a dove.

TREAT TO EAT: Locusts for Lunch!

Mix equal parts of peanut butter and powdered sugar to make dough. Give each child a small chunk of dough and two sliced almonds. Show children how to roll the dough into a ball, then push the end of each almond into it to form wings. Explain that John lived in the desert and ate bugs called locusts.

✔ Before preparing the snacks, check to make sure children are not allergic to the ingredients.

STORY PICTURE: Jesus Is Baptized

Give each child a copy of the "Today I Learned..." handout (p. 121). Place glue, crayons, and clear cellophane on the table. Let the children color the water, then glue cellophane to it for added shine. As the children are working, talk about how the voice from heaven and the dove showed how much God loved Jesus.

Jesus did what was right.

TODAY I LEARNED...

The Point ✎ Jesus did what was right and pleased God.

Today your child learned that Jesus did what was right and pleased God. They heard that Jesus went to John to be baptized. Children talked about ways they can please God this week.

Verse to Learn

"Do what is right and good in the Lord's sight" (Deuteronomy 6:18a).

Ask Me...

- What happened when Jesus was baptized?
- How did God show that he loved Jesus?
- How do you think our family pleases God?

Family Fun

- Using sugar-cookie dough, bake dove-shaped cookies. Throughout the week give your children dove cookies when they do something right and you are pleased with them. Affirm them for living right like Jesus.

Jesus Is Baptized (Matthew 3:13-17)

Tempting Troubles

The Point

✏️ Jesus did what was right even when it was hard.

The Bible Basis

Matthew 4:1-11. Jesus is tempted in the wilderness.

After Jesus' baptism, God proclaimed that Jesus was his Son. Satan sought to disrupt the relationship between Father and Son by tempting Jesus with three challenges. The temptation to turn stones to bread might have caused Jesus to doubt his Father's care and provision during a time of fasting. The temptation to leap from the Temple could have been to see if Jesus would force God to act, rather than simply trusting in God's protection. The last temptation, an offer of all the kingdoms of the world, tested Jesus' loyalty to God. In each case, Jesus prevailed over Satan, using God's Word as a shield, citing verses from Deuteronomy 6 and 8.

The 5- and 6-year-olds in your class have experienced temptation. They know about the urge to sneak to the cookie jar, the desire to disobey, and that mysterious pull that entices a child to take a toy from a friend's house. Children can understand that temptation isn't sin unless they give in to it. Use this lesson to help your students understand that when they face temptation, they can use God's Word and choose to do what's right, just as Jesus did.

Getting the Point

✏️ **Jesus did what was right even when it was hard.**

It's important to say The Point just as it's written in each activity. Repeating The Point over and over will help the children remember it and apply it to their lives.

Children will
- experience the pull of temptation,
- discover that Jesus overcame temptation,
- help Pockets do the right thing, and
- learn that they can do the right thing, even when it's hard.

🖊️ **The Point**

This Lesson at a Glance

Before the lesson, collect the necessary items for the activities you plan to use. Refer to the Classroom Supplies and Learning Lab Supplies columns to determine what you'll need. Remember to make photocopies of the "Today I Learned..." handout (p. 133) to send home with your children.

Section	Minutes	What Children Will Do	Classroom Supplies	Learning Lab Supplies
Welcome Time	up to 5	**Welcome!**—Receive name tags and be greeted by the teacher.	"Star Name Tags" handouts (p. 30), markers, pins or tape	
Let's Get Started Direct children to one or more of the Let's Get Started activities until everyone arrives.	up to 10	**Option 1: Bible Shields**—Create shields to resist temptation.	Paper plates, markers, crayons, stapler, fabric	Thumbs Up stamp and ink pad
	up to 10	**Option 2: Wild Wilderness**—Design pictures from natural items.	Construction paper, glue, sand or sandpaper, rocks, leaves, sticks	
	up to 10	**Option 3: Tempting Treats**—Make cinnamon biscuits.	Cinnamon sugar, refrigerator biscuits, butter, cookie sheets	
Pick-Up Song	up to 5	**We Will Pick Up**—Sing a song as they pick up toys and gather for Bible-Story Time.	CD player	CD: "We Will Pick Up" (track 2)
Bible-Story Time	up to 5	**Setting the Stage**—Use paper shields to "battle temptation."	Shields from Option 1, newspaper, masking tape	
	up to 5	**Bible Song and Prayer Time**—Sing a song, bring out the Bible, and pray together.	Bible, construction paper, scissors, basket or box, CD player	Thumbs Up stamp and ink pad, CD: "God's Book" (track 3)
	up to 10	**Hear the Bible Story**—Cheer for Jesus as he overcomes each temptation in Matthew 4:1-11.	CD player, shields from Option 1	Learning Mat: Story Circle 4, CD: "Jesus Says No!" (track 17)
	up to 10	**Do the Bible Story**—Resist pushing and pulling trio members.	Masking tape	Egg timer
Practicing the Point	up to 5	**Puzzled Pockets**—Help Pockets learn the importance of resisting temptation.	Pockets the Kangaroo, coins, CD player	CD: "I Love Jesus" (track 16)
Closing	up to 5	**Victory Cheer**—Enjoy a treat they've resisted and perform a victory cheer.	Cinnamon biscuits from Option 3	
For Extra Time		For extra-time ideas and supplies, see page 132.		

Jesus did what was right.

Welcome Time

Welcome! (up to 5 minutes)

● Bend down and make eye contact with children as they arrive.
● Greet each child individually with an enthusiastic smile.
● Thank each child for coming to class today.
● As children arrive, ask them about last week's "Today I Learned..." discussion. Ask questions such as "How did Jesus please God?" and "What did you do this past week that pleased God?"
● Say: **Today we're going to learn that** **Jesus did what was right even when it was hard.**
● Hand out the star name tags children made in the first lesson and help them attach the name tags to their clothing. If some of the name tags were damaged or if some of the children weren't in class that week, have them make new name tags using the photocopiable patterns on page 30.
● Direct children to the Let's Get Started activities you've set up.

◗ The Point

Let's Get Started

Set up one or more of the following activities for children to do as they arrive. After you greet each child, invite him or her to choose an activity.

Circulate among the children to offer help as needed and direct children's conversation toward today's lesson. Ask questions such as "What things are hard to resist?" and "When have you really wanted something you know you shouldn't have?"

▢ Option 1: Bible Shields (up to 10 minutes)

Before children arrive, cut enough 1×4-inch strips of fabric for each child to have one.

Set out paper plates, markers, crayons, a stapler, the fabric strips, and the *Thumbs Up stamp and ink pad.* Allow children to decorate the back of a paper plate to look like a shield, then staple the ends of a fabric strip to the front as a handle. Have children make extra shields for those who don't choose this option. Tell children that today's story is about a time when Jesus used God's Word to protect himself from temptation. Children will use the shields during the "Setting the Stage" activity.

▢ Option 2: Wild Wilderness (up to 10 minutes)

Set out construction paper, glue, and sandpaper or bowls of sand. Lead children outside to collect sticks, leaves, flowers, small stones, and bits of grass.

 ✔ If bad weather keeps you from going outside, bring silk flowers and leaves to class.

Inside your classroom, help children use the items they've gathered to make wilderness scenes. Demonstrate how to glue sand or sandpaper to the bottom half of the paper to represent the dry, sandy desert floor. As children are working, explain that Jesus went through a hard time in the wilderness.

OPTION 3: Tempting Treats (up to 10 minutes)

Set out refrigerator biscuits, a bowl of cinnamon sugar, a bowl of melted butter or margarine, and a cookie sheet. Help children dip the biscuits in butter, then in cinnamon sugar, and place the treats on a greased cookie sheet. As children work, talk about how delicious the treats smell and how wonderful they'll taste. Tell children that it's not time to eat the biscuits, but they sure are tempting! Explain that today they'll hear a story about a time when Jesus was tempted. Have an adult helper bake the biscuits according to package directions. Allow the treats to cool in your classroom, where children can see and smell them.

When everyone has arrived and you're ready to move on to the Bible-Story Time, encourage the children to finish what they're doing and get ready to clean up.

Pick-Up Song

We Will Pick Up (up to 5 minutes)

Lead children in singing "We Will Pick Up" (track 2) with the *CD* to the tune of "London Bridge." Encourage children to sing along as they help clean up the room.

If you want to include the names of all the children in your class, sing the song without the *CD* and repeat the naming section. If you choose to use the *CD,* vary the names you use each week.

Sing

We will pick up all our toys,
All our toys, all our toys.
We will pick up all our toys
And put them all away.

I see (name) picking up,
Picking up, picking up.
I see (name) picking up
And putting toys away.

(Repeat.)

Bible-Story Time

Setting the Stage (up to 5 minutes)

Tell the children you'll clap your hands to get their attention. Explain that when you clap, the children are to stop what they're doing, raise their hands, and focus on you. Encourage children to respond quickly so you'll have time

Jesus did what was right.

for all the fun activities you've planned.

Before class, make a masking tape line down the middle of the room. Form two groups and have the groups stand on opposite sides of the line.

Give each child three sheets of newspaper and a shield from Option 1. Have children wad their newspapers into three paper balls. Say: **When I say "go," you can throw your paper balls at the other group. But be careful! At the same time you'll use your shield to protect yourself from the other group's paper balls. After you've thrown your three balls, sit against this wall and wait for others to finish. You may be tempted to pick up extra balls and throw them, too. But remember, you don't want to give in to temptation! Ready? Go!**

When everyone has had a chance to throw their three balls, form a circle. Ask:

● **What was it like to have paper balls thrown at you?** (Scary; weird; hard to keep away from them; fun.)

● **Was it easy to shield yourself from the paper? Explain.** (Yes, because no one threw at me; yes, because I was watching for people to throw at me.)

● **Was it hard to shield yourself from the paper? Explain.** (Yes, because there were so many papers flying around; yes, because my shield wasn't very big.)

Say: **Today we're going to hear about a time when Jesus had to protect himself from Satan. Jesus used God's Word as a shield to resist Satan's temptations. In our story, we'll see that ✏ Jesus did what was right even when it was hard. First, we need to clean up our "battleground." You might be tempted to throw another paper ball, but try very hard to resist! Let's put the paper in the garbage can, instead.**

Help children clean up the newspaper before moving on to the next activity.

Bible Song and Prayer Time (up to 5 minutes)

Before class, make surprise cards for this activity by cutting construction paper into 2×6-inch slips. Prepare a surprise card for each child, plus a few extras for visitors. Fold the cards in half, then stamp the *Thumbs Up stamp* inside one of the surprise cards. Mark Matthew 4:1-11 in the Bible you'll be using.

Have children sit in a circle. Say: **Now it's time to choose a Bible person to bring me the Bible marked with today's Bible story. As we sing our Bible song, I'll pass out the surprise cards. Don't look inside your surprise card until the song is over.**

Lead children in singing "God's Book" (track 3) with the *CD* to the tune of "Old MacDonald Had a Farm." As you sing, pass out the folded surprise cards. If you want to include the names of all the children in your class, sing the song without the *CD* and repeat the naming section. If you choose to use the *CD*, vary the names you use each week.

✏ **The Point**

Sing 🎵

Now it's time to read God's Book	**(Name)'s here.**
And hear a Bible story.	**(Name)'s here.**
It's fun to be here with my	**Here is (name).**
friends	**Here is (name).**
And hear a Bible story.	**Now it's time to read God's Book**
	And hear a Bible story.

Jesus did what was right.

Now it's time to read God's Book	(Name)'s here.
And hear a Bible story.	(Name)'s here.
It's fun to be here with my	Here is (name).
friends	Here is (name).
And hear a Bible story.	Now it's time to read God's Book
	And hear a Bible story.

After the song, say: **You may look inside your surprise cards. The person who has the Thumbs Up stamped inside his or her card will be our Bible person for today.**

Identify the Bible person, then have the rest of the children clap for him or her. Ask the Bible person to bring you the Bible. Help the Bible person open the Bible to the marked place and show children where your story comes from. Then have the Bible person sit down.

● **The Point**

Say: (Name) **was our special Bible person today. Each week, we'll have only one special Bible person, but each one of you is a special part of our class! Today we're all learning that ● Jesus did what was right even when it was hard.**

Let's say a special prayer now and ask God to help us do what is right even when it's hard. I'll pass around this basket. When the basket comes to you, put your surprise card in it and say, "God, help me do what is right even when it's hard."

Pass around the basket or box. When you've collected everyone's surprise card, set the basket aside and pick up the Bible. Lead children in this prayer: **God, thank you for the Bible and all the stories in it. Teach us today that ● Jesus did what was right even when it was hard. Amen.**

● **The Point**

Hear the Bible Story (up to 10 minutes)

Bring out the *Learning Mat: Story Circle 4* and tape the ends together to form a circle. Have children gather around you with their shields from Option 1. Say: **Our Bible story comes from the book of Matthew in the Bible. Our *Story Circle* shows us pictures of our Bible story. Today you'll hear about someone named Satan, or the devil. Satan is God's enemy. God wants us to do what's right, but Satan tries to get us to do what's wrong. That's called temptation. As you listen to the story on the *CD*, hold up your shield and give your neighbor a high five each time Jesus overcomes Satan's temptation. Listen carefully!**

Hold up *Story Circle 4* so children can see the first scene. Play "Jesus Says No!" (track 17) on the *CD*. Each time you hear the chime, move the *Story Circle* so children can see the next scene of the story.

When the track ends, turn off the CD player and put *Story Circle 4* out of sight. Ask:

● **Where did Satan tempt Jesus?** (In the desert; on the Temple; on a mountain.)

● **How did Jesus resist Satan's temptations?** (By quoting Bible verses; by knowing what God's Word said; he was stronger than Satan.)

● **Why would Satan want to tempt Jesus?** (To make Jesus not love God; to take Jesus away from God; to make himself more powerful.)

● **Why does Satan want to tempt us today?** (So we'll do wrong things; so we'll turn away from God; to keep us from loving God.)

Say: **Satan doesn't want us to love God. That's why he tries to pull us away with tempting things. But**  **Jesus did what was right even when it was hard—and so can you! By knowing what the Bible says and by calling on God, we can turn away from those bad things and choose to do what's right. Let's see what it's like to resist the pull of temptation.**

Do the Bible Story (up to 10 minutes)

Before this activity, use masking tape to make one X on the floor for every three children.

Form trios and send each trio to an X. Instruct each trio to choose a Resister, who will stand on the X with his or her eyes closed. Have the other two members be Temptations and stand on either side with a hand on the Resister's shoulder. Say: **When I start the *egg timer,* the Temptations will try to push and pull their Resisters off the X. Temptations must have their feet planted in one place so they don't move around, and they can only push and pull with one hand. If a Resister steps off the X, he or she may step back on and try again until time runs out. Then trade places and allow one of the Temptations to be the Resister. Ready?**

Turn over the *egg timer* and start the game. Play three rounds to give each person an opportunity to be a Resister. Then gather children together and ask:

● **What was hard about being a Resister?** (I couldn't see when they were going to push me; I couldn't stay on the X; they were pushing and pulling so much, I got tired.)

Say: **Just like it was hard to resist the pull of your trio members, it's hard to resist the pull of temptation. Sometimes we can't see where temptations will come from, and sometimes they're pretty strong. Fortunately, God's Word is stronger than any temptations we'll face! Jesus used verses from the Bible to help him do what was right, even when it was hard. God's Word reminded him that God is more powerful than anything.** Ask:

● **How can you do what's right, even when it's hard?** (Remember the Bible; pray; ask for help from my mom; walk away.)

Say: **Those are super ways to resist the temptation to do wrong! Maybe you can share your ideas with Pockets when she comes to visit today. Let's call and see if she's around. Pockets! Pockets!**

Practicing the Point

Puzzled Pockets (up to 5 minutes)

Place several coins in Pockets' pouch.

Bring out Pockets the Kangaroo and go through the following puppet script. When you finish the script, put Pockets away and out of sight.

Puzzled Pockets

PUPPET SCRIPT

Pockets: (*Enters, bouncing and jingling the change in her pouch.*) Hi, everyone! Sorry I'm late. My mommy was giving me my allowance. I love to hear it jingle . . . but sometimes I wish there were more coins to jingle!

Teacher: Why?

Pockets: (*Stops jingling.*) Well, you see, there's this super cool sticker book that my friend Sarah has. I'd really, really, REALLY like to have one, but it costs a lot of money. So I've been saving my allowance for two weeks so I can buy the sticker book.

Teacher: Pockets, I'm proud that you're saving your money. That can be very hard!

Pockets: (*Sighs.*) Boy, do I know it! The other day when I went to look at the sticker book, there was no one around in the store. So I took the book off the shelf and held it in my hands for a little while. Since no one was looking, I thought how easy it would be to put the book in my pouch and hop out of the store.

Teacher: Hmmm. Sounds like you were fighting the temptation to do something wrong, Pockets.

Pockets: (*Sighs.*) I know. I want that sticker book and it's taking sooo long to save for it. That day in the store, I almost stole it.

Teacher: So you didn't take the sticker book? What stopped you?

Pockets: I remembered that the Bible said not to steal. And taking the book would have been stealing. So I put it back and left.

Teacher: (*Hugs Pockets.*) Good for you, Pockets! You did the right thing, even though it must have been hard! We've just been talking about how Jesus fought temptation, too. Who'd like to tell Pockets what Jesus did? (*Allow children to share about Jesus' resisting Satan's temptations. Be sure they tell Pockets that Jesus used God's Word to resist Satan.*)

Pockets: Wow! That must have been hard for Jesus just like it was hard for me. But we both did the right things!

Teacher: I am so proud of you, Pockets! You know what? I feel like singing, and I know just the song. Children, let's teach Pockets the song we learned about doing right, as Jesus did.

Lead children and Pockets in singing "I Love Jesus" (track 16) to the tune of "London Bridge" with the *CD*.

Jesus did what was right.

Sing

Jesus did just what was right,	I can try to do what's right,
Every day,	Every day,
Every night.	Every night.
He was pleasing in God's sight.	I'll be pleasing in God's sight—
I love Jesus!	I love Jesus!

TODAY I LEARNED . . .

We believe that Christian education extends beyond the classroom into the home. Photocopy the "Today I Learned . . ." handout (p. 133) for this week and send it home with your children. Encourage parents to use the handout to plan meaningful family activities to reinforce this week's topic. Follow up the "Today I Learned . . ." activities next week by asking children what their families did.

Closing

Victory Cheer (up to 5 minutes)

Say: **Pockets did the right thing, even though it wasn't easy. We can do the right things, too, no matter how hard they are!** Hold up the cinnamon biscuits or some other treat. **You've all done a hard thing by resisting these tempting, tasty treats. Now it's time to enjoy them together!**

Distribute the treats and allow children to eat them. Then say: **Let's close with a cheer to celebrate the fact that ◉Jesus did the right thing even when it was hard. I'll tell you what Satan said, then you'll all say, "Jesus said, 'No way!'"**

Satan said, "Turn these stones to bread."
Jesus said, "No way!"
"Jump from the Temple," Satan said.
Jesus said, "No way!"
Satan said, "Bow and worship me!"
Jesus said, "No way!"
Jesus claimed a victory—
'Cause Jesus said, "No way!"

◉ **The Point**

For Extra Time

If you have a long class time or want to add additional elements to your lesson, try one of the following activities.

LIVELY LEARNING: *Story Circle* Listening Center

Let your children enjoy listening to the stories of Jesus doing right as he grew up. Tape all four *Learning Mat: Story Circles* together to make one large circle that children can turn around as they listen to the *CD*. Set the *Story Circle* and the CD player in a corner of the room. The entire story of "Jesus Grows Up" is track 18 on the *CD*. (There are chimes for the last three *Story Circles* that indicate when to turn the circles.)

MAKE TO TAKE: Care Cards

● **The Point**

Set out paper, glitter glue, sequins, crayons, markers, and glue. Explain that the angels came and cared for Jesus when he was tired and hungry. Have children design Care Cards for friends or family members who might be feeling sad. As children work, remind them that ● Jesus did what was right even when it was hard. Tell them that their Care Cards might give people the encouragement they need to do the right things even when it's hard.

TREAT TO EAT: Victory Bread

Give each child a slice of bread. Allow each child to use honey from a squeeze bottle to draw a happy face on the bread. Explain that God is pleased when we say no to temptation.

STORY PICTURE: Jesus Overcomes Temptation

Give each child a copy of the "Today I Learned . . ." handout (p. 133). Set out glue sticks, glue, a container of ground cinnamon, and crayons. After children have colored their pictures, let them spread glue onto the desert ground and sprinkle cinnamon on top. As children are working, remind them that Jesus stood strong against temptation and used God's Word to defeat the devil.

Jesus did what was right.

TODAY I LEARNED . . .

The Point ✏ Jesus did what was right even when it was hard.

LESSON 9

Today your child learned that Jesus did what was right even when it was hard. Children discovered that Jesus resisted Satan's temptation in a very difficult time. They talked about how they can resist temptation and choose to do what is right.

Verse to Learn

"Do what is right and good in the Lord's sight" (Deuteronomy 6:18a).

Ask Me . . .

● What did Jesus use to resist Satan?

● How can God's Word help you do the right thing?

● What hard things does our family face? How can God's Word help us through them?

Family Fun

● Think of temptations that your child faces, such as disobeying, lying, or being unkind. Toss a paper wad at your child and say a tempting situation like, "Not cleaning your room." Let your child use a Bible or a paper plate to shield himself or herself from the paper. Then allow your child to throw paper wads as you protect yourself with a Bible. Use this game to teach your child verses such as Deuteronomy 6:18a or James 4:7b.

Jesus Overcomes Temptation (Matthew 4:1-11)

Jesus Is With Us

The disciples lived as Jesus' closest companions for three years. They witnessed his amazing miracles, heard his powerful teaching, and saw lives transformed by his love. We can only imagine the disciples' sadness when Jesus announced that he would soon return to his Father. But Jesus offered this comforting promise: "And surely I am with you always, to the very end of the age" (Matthew 28:20b). Just as he'd welcomed the little children, comforted the lonely Samaritan woman, calmed his frightened disciples, and brought joy to Jairus' family, Jesus promised to be with his followers forever!

Jesus' promise still holds true today. As increasingly independent 5- and 6-year-olds begin to venture outside the comfort zone of a safe and familiar home, they need to know that they can count on Jesus being with them. Some go to school, spend the night at friends' houses, and join sports teams. This newfound freedom can be both exciting and frightening. Children may find themselves feeling lonely, scared, or sad when they're out on their own. You can offer children the comfort of a Savior who promises to be with them always! Use these lessons to help children understand that Jesus will always be with them.

Four Lessons on Jesus Is With Us

	Page	Point	Bible Basis
Lesson 10 **All the Time**	141	Jesus is with us all the time.	Matthew 18:1-5, 10; 19:13-15
Lesson 11 **Never Alone**	153	Jesus is with us when we're lonely.	John 4:4-30, 39
Lesson 12 **Fear Not!**	165	Jesus is with us when we're afraid.	Matthew 8:23-27
Lesson 13 **Sad Face, Glad Face**	179	Jesus is with us when we're sad.	Luke 8:40-42, 49-56

Time Stretchers

Jesus Sees Me Always

Teach children "Jesus Sees You" to the tune of "Frère Jacques." This song is not on the *CD*. Form pairs and have partners face each other. Explain that one partner will lead and the other will echo the song and motions.

Jesus sees you *(touch fingertips together to make glasses)*
Jesus sees you *(touch fingertips together to make glasses)*
All the time. *(Tap wrist.)*
All the time. *(Tap wrist.)*
Even when you're _____ *(pantomime action),*
Even when you're _____ *(pantomime action),*
He is there! *(Clap on each word.)*
He is there! *(Clap on each word.)*

Children may fill in the blank with actions such as eating, sleeping, dancing, playing, sleeping, or smiling.

A Visible Reminder

Set out toothpicks and bowls of lemon juice. Distribute sheets of paper and have children use cotton swabs to draw simple pictures with lemon juice. When children have finished, point out the fact that it looks like their drawings aren't there. When the juice is dry, have children hold their papers close to a warm light bulb for a few moments. They'll be delighted to see their invisible pictures suddenly become visible! Explain that even though we don't see Jesus, he's always there.

Buddies

Form pairs and give each pair a bandanna or scarf. Use the bandannas to help partners tie their legs together, as if they were going to compete in a three-legged race. Allow pairs to take turns walking, hopping, or tiptoeing around. Explain that Jesus is with us when we play, when we run, and when we sleep. He's like our closest friend!

Remembering God's Word

Each four- or five-week module focuses on a key Bible verse. The key verse for this module is "I am with you always, to the very end of the age" (Matthew 28:20b).

This module's key verse will teach children that Jesus is with them always. Have fun using these ideas any time during the lessons on "Jesus is with us."

Cheerleaders

Show children how to roll up sheets of paper and tape them securely to make megaphones. Form two groups and have them stand on opposite sides of the room, facing each other. Encourage children to use their megaphones as you lead them in the following verse.

Group 1: **I am with you always,**
Group 2: **I am with you always,**
Group 2: **To the very end of the age.**
Group 1: **To the very end of the age.**
Group 1: **Matthew 28:20b.**
Group 2: **Matthew 28:20b.**
Group 2: **I am with you always,**
Group 1: **To the very end of the age.**
All: **Matthew 28:20b.**

Circle of Jesus' Love

Have children sit in a circle on the floor. Walk around the outside of the circle, tapping children's heads, as in the game Duck, Duck, Goose. As you tap each child's head, say a word from the first portion of Matthew 28:20b. **I...am...with...you...always.** When you say the word "always," have that child stand up, hold your hand, and skip around the circle with you. Then sit in that child's place and allow him or her to continue to say the verse and tap other children. After each child has had a turn to skip around the circle with a partner, say: **Jesus is with us just as our partners were when we skipped around the circle.**

Story Enhancements

Make Bible stories come alive in your classroom by bringing in Bible costumes, setting out sensory items, or creating bulletin boards. When children learn with their five senses as well as with their hearts and minds, lessons come alive and are remembered. Each week bring in one or more items to help involve and motivate children in the Bible lessons they'll be learning. The following ideas will help you get started.

"Jesus Is With Me" Bulletin Board

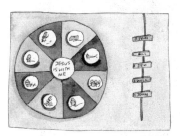

Create this fun "Jesus Is With Me" bulletin board in your classroom. Cut a 2-foot circle out of poster board and divide it into eight sections. Color each section differently, or cut sheets of colored construction paper to fit each section and glue them in place.

Make enlarged photocopies of the "All the Time" handout (p. 139). Cut out the pictures, invite children to color them, and glue them on different sections of the circle. Then write "Jesus Is With Me" on a smaller circle and place it in the middle of the large circle. Staple the colorful circle on your bulletin board, leaving the edges free. Let children write their names on clothespins and clip them to a string you've attached to your board.

As children come to class each week, encourage them to clip their clothespins to the pictures that tell where they knew that Jesus was with them during the week.

Lesson 10

● Before class, trace the hand prints of several adults. Then allow children to trace their own hand prints and compare them to the larger ones. Remind children that even though they may be small, Jesus thinks they're very important.

● Bring in your school yearbooks from elementary school through high school or college. As children look at the people, explain that Jesus is with us as we grow and change.

Lesson 11

● Bring in a pitcher of ice-cold water and let children pour themselves drinks. Talk about how nice the water feels and tastes when we're very thirsty. Explain that Jesus offered the woman at the well something more refreshing and wonderful than water.

● Set out picture books of Israel and the surrounding areas. As you point out the dry, dusty climate, explain that the woman at the well would be very happy to hear about water that would quench her thirst forever.

Lesson 12

● Bring in a 2-liter soft drink container filled with water, 1/4 cup of vegetable oil, and a few drops of blue food coloring. Slip a plastic toy boat or small piece of wood in the container before closing the lid tightly. Allow children to shake the container to make a storm. Point out that the disciples would be very frightened by the tall waves and wind.

● Fill a dishpan with water and place it outside. Have two children work together to push and pull the dishpan and make waves. Then instruct them to stop moving the dishpan so the water becomes still. Explain that Jesus calmed the water with just a word.

Lesson 13

● With a cassette recorder, record each child laughing. Then play the tape back and see if children can pick out each other's laughter.

● Bring in pictures of sad people from magazines and newspapers. Have children think of reasons why the people would be sad. Remind children that Jesus is with us when we're sad.

All the Time

Make enlarged photocopies of the figures. Allow children to cut out and color the figures.

All the Time

The Point

🖊 Jesus is with us all the time.

The Bible Basis

Matthew 18:1-5, 10; 19:13-15. Jesus welcomes the children.

It's hard to believe that Jesus' disciples argued about who was the greatest. These men who had followed Jesus, heard his teachings, witnessed his miracles, and knew him as the Son of God, were still jockeying for a higher position in God's kingdom. They were being selfish, immature, and foolish. Jesus' response taught them what it meant to be childlike—trusting, humble, and innocent. He cautioned the disciples to value children, look to their example of faith and humility, and follow it.

The 5- and 6-year-olds in your class need constant affirmation. Adults often talk down to children and make them feel inadequate, unimportant, and small. But Jesus was quick to show his love for children. He welcomed them, blessed them, and praised their tender and trusting hearts. It's essential that children realize their value in Jesus' eyes—that he loves them and will be there all the time. Use this lesson to show your students that Jesus loves them so much he watches them night and day.

Getting the Point

🖊 **Jesus is with us all the time.**

It's important to say The Point just as it's written in each activity. Repeating The Point over and over will help the children remember it and apply it to their lives.

Children will
- learn that Jesus is with them all the time,
- discover that Jesus said children were important, and
- remind each other that Jesus is with them throughout the day.

🖊 **The Point**

This Lesson at a Glance

Before the lesson, collect the necessary items for the activities you plan to use. Refer to the Classroom Supplies and Learning Lab Supplies columns to determine what you'll need. Remember to make photocopies of the "Today I Learned..." handout (p. 152) to send home with your children.

Section	Minutes	What Children Will Do	Classroom Supplies	Learning Lab Supplies
Welcome Time	up to 5	**Welcome!**—Receive name tags and be greeted by the teacher.	"Star Name Tags" handouts (p. 30), markers, pins or tape	
Let's Get Started Direct children to one or more of the Let's Get Started activities until everyone arrives.	up to 10	**Option 1: All the Children**—Decorate the classroom with paper-chain children.	Crayons, scissors, "All the Children" handout (p. 151)	
	up to 10	**Option 2: Angels Watchin' Over Me**—Make guardian angels.	Newsprint, crayons, tape or stapler	
	up to 10	**Option 3: Copy Cats**—Imitate their partners' actions.		
Pick-Up Song	up to 5	**We Will Pick Up**—Sing a song as they pick up toys and gather for Bible-Story Time.	CD player	CD: "We Will Pick Up" (track 2)
Bible-Story Time	up to 5	**Setting the Stage**—Play a game and act as guardian angels.	Newspaper	Egg timer
	up to 5	**Bible Song and Prayer Time**—Sing a song, bring out the Bible, and pray together.	Bible, construction paper, scissors, basket or box, CD player	CD: "God's Book" (track 3), Jesus and Me stamp and ink pad
	up to 10	**Hear the Bible Story**—Travel through a special obstacle course, then listen to Matthew 18:1-5, 10; 19:13-15 to hear how Jesus welcomed children.	Bible	Bible Big Book: Jesus Is With Us
	up to 10	**Do the Bible Story**—Play a game and share times when Jesus is with them.	Yarn or string, masking tape, "All the Time" handout (p. 139), CD player	CD: "Walk Around the Clock" (track 19)
Practicing the Point	up to 5	**Missing Mommy**—Help Pockets realize that Jesus is with her all the time.	Pockets the Kangaroo	
Closing	up to 5	**Open Your Eyes!**—Sing a song and tell where they'll look for Jesus this week.	CD player	CD: "Jesus Is Always There" (track 20)
For Extra Time	For extra-time ideas and supplies, see page 150.			

Jesus is with us.

Welcome Time

Welcome! (up to 5 minutes)

- Bend down and make eye contact with children as they arrive.
- Greet each child individually with an enthusiastic smile.
- Thank each child for coming to class today.
- As children arrive, ask them about last week's "Today I Learned…" discussion. Ask questions such as "What hard things did you face this week?" and "How did Jesus help you do the right thing?"
- Say: **Today we're going to learn that ◐ Jesus is with us all the time.**
- Hand out the star name tags children made in the first lesson and help them attach the name tags to their clothing. If some of the name tags were damaged or if some of the children weren't in class that week, have them make new name tags using the photocopiable patterns on page 30.
- Direct children to the Let's Get Started activities you've set up.

◐ The Point

Let's Get Started

Set up one or more of the following activities for children to do as they arrive. After you greet each child, invite him or her to choose an activity.

Circulate among the children to offer help as needed and direct children's conversation toward today's lesson. Ask questions such as "When is Jesus with you?" or "Do you think children are important?"

☐ OPTION 1: All the Children (up to 10 minutes)

Set out scissors, crayons, and photocopies of the "All the Children" handout (p. 151). Help children fold the handout on the dotted lines, then cut along the solid lines to make two children holding hands. Allow children to cut out and decorate as many "paper pairs" as they'd like. You may want to have children tape them around the edge of a bulletin board or window. Explain that in today's story, they'll learn that Jesus loved children very much!

☐ OPTION 2: Angels Watchin' Over Me (up to 10 minutes)

Set out crayons and large sheets of newsprint. Have pairs take turns tracing each other as one partner lies on a sheet of newsprint with arms and legs outstretched. Explain that they're each making a special angel. Help them create wings and a robe by drawing an arc from wrist to waist, and between children's feet (see diagram). Allow children to decorate their angels and tape or staple them to the wall. Explain that God's angels watch over us all the time.

☐ OPTION 3: Copy Cats (up to 10 minutes)

Form pairs and have partners face each other. Tell children that the shorter partners will be the Cats and the taller partners will be the Copy Cats. Have the Cats move slowly, doing simple motions, such as putting their arms up, standing on tiptoe, crouching down, or making silly faces. Instruct the Copy Cats to imitate their partners' motions, as if they're looking in a mirror. You may want to play upbeat music to help children think of unique motions. After a minute or so, have partners switch roles. Explain that just as the Copy Cats stayed with their partners, Jesus stays with us all the time.

When everyone has arrived and you're ready to move on to the Bible-Story Time, encourage the children to finish what they're doing and get ready to clean up.

Pick-Up Song

We Will Pick Up (up to 5 minutes)

Lead children in singing "We Will Pick Up" (track 2) with the *CD* to the tune of "London Bridge." Encourage children to sing along as they help clean up the room.

If you want to include the names of all the children in your class, sing the song without the *CD* and repeat the naming section. If you choose to use the *CD*, vary the names you use each week.

Sing

We will pick up all our toys,	**I see** (name) **picking up,**
All our toys, all our toys.	**Picking up, picking up.**
We will pick up all our toys	**I see** (name) **picking up**
And put them all away.	**And putting toys away.**
	(Repeat.)

Bible-Story Time

Setting the Stage (up to 5 minutes)

Tell the children you'll clap your hands to get their attention. Explain that when you clap, the children are to stop what they're doing, raise their hands, and focus on you. Encourage children to respond quickly so you'll have time for all the fun activities you've planned.

Choose one child to be "It" and have him or her wad up several sheets of newspaper. Then form groups of four and have each group form a circle around one of its members. Say: **If you're in the middle, you're surrounded by your Guardian Angels. They'll protect you from It. It will have 30 seconds to tag you with a newspaper ball. But It can't tag any Guardian Angels. The Guardian Angels will gently pull you away from It and form a wall to keep It from tagging you. Are you ready?**

Turn over the *egg timer* and begin the game. When time runs out, have

Jesus is with us.

groups change roles so a different child is in the middle. Choose a new child to be It for each round. After four rounds, gather children and ask:

● **What made it hard for It to tag you?** (The Guardian Angels; my friends around me; It couldn't get to me)

● **What was it like to be in the middle?** (Exciting; I felt safe; I knew nothing could get to me.)

● **What would it be like to always be protected this way?** (Great; fun; weird; I'd always be safe.)

Say: **Our game gave us an idea of what it might be like to have angels protecting us. Did you know that God sends his angels to watch over each of us? He does! Today we'll learn that** ● **Jesus is with us all the time. Let's get ready to hear how important children are to Jesus.**

Bible Song and Prayer Time (up to 5 minutes)

Before class, make surprise cards for this activity by cutting construction paper into 2×6-inch slips. Prepare a surprise card for each child, plus a few extras for visitors. Fold the cards in half, then stamp the *Jesus and Me stamp* inside one of the surprise cards. Mark Matthew 18:1-5, 10; 19:13-15 in the Bible you'll be using.

Have children sit in a circle. Say: **Now it's time to choose a Bible person to bring me the Bible marked with today's Bible story. As we sing our Bible song, I'll pass out the surprise cards. Don't look inside your surprise card until the song is over.**

Lead children in singing "God's Book" (track 3) with the *CD* to the tune of "Old MacDonald Had a Farm." As you sing, pass out the folded surprise cards. If you want to include the names of all the children in your class, sing the song without the *CD* and repeat the naming section. If you choose to use the *CD*, vary the names you use each week.

● **The Point**

If the ink pad is dry, moisten it with three to five drops of water.

Sing

Now it's time to read God's Book	Now it's time to read God's Book
And hear a Bible story.	And hear a Bible story.
It's fun to be here with my friends	It's fun to be here with my friends
And hear a Bible story.	And hear a Bible story.
(Name)**'s here.**	(Name)**'s here.**
(Name)**'s here.**	(Name)**'s here.**
Here is (name).	**Here is** (name).
Here is (name).	**Here is** (name).
Now it's time to read God's Book	**Now it's time to read God's Book**
And hear a Bible story.	**And hear a Bible story.**

After the song, say: **You may look inside your surprise cards. The person who has the picture of Jesus stamped inside his or her card will be our Bible person for today.**

Identify the Bible person, then have the rest of the children clap for him or her. Ask the Bible person to bring you the Bible. Help the Bible person open the Bible to the marked place and show children where your story comes from. Then have the Bible person sit down.

⬤ The Point

Say: (Name) **was our special Bible person today. Each week, we'll have only one special Bible person, but each one of you is a special part of our class! Today we're all learning that** ⬤ **Jesus is with us all the time.**

Let's say a special prayer now and ask God to be with us today. I'll pass around this basket. When the basket comes to you, put your surprise card in it and say, "God, be with me now."

Pass around the basket or box. When you've collected everyone's surprise card, set the basket aside and pick up the Bible. Lead children in this prayer: **God, thank you for the Bible and all the stories in it. Teach us today that** ⬤ **Jesus is with us all the time. Amen.**

⬤ The Point

Hear the Bible Story (up to 10 minutes)

Before class, set up a comfortable story area in one corner of your room with pillows, blankets, or carpet squares. Then set up a "kid-friendly" obstacle course that leads to the story area. Have children climb over and under tables and chairs. You might want to hang streamers between two tables or chairs to make a low entrance to the story area.

Gather children at the opposite end of the room and say: **I've set up a special, comfortable story area for us to enjoy today. But to reach the story area, you'll have to go through an obstacle course made just for you!** Point out the obstacle course. **Even though it's just your size, I'll try the obstacle course, too.** Help children make their way through the course and gather at the story area. Be sure they watch as you struggle through the small spaces and low areas of the course. When you've reached the story area, ask:

● **Why was it easier for you to enter the story area than for me?** (Because we're all small; we could fit under the table and chairs.)

Say: **Because you're children and you're smaller than I am, you had an easier time getting to the story area. Today we'll hear why Jesus' friends needed to be like children.** Point to the Bible and say: **Our story comes from the book of Matthew in the Bible.** Hold up the *Bible Big Book: Jesus Is With Us.* **Our Bible Big Book shows us pictures of our Bible story.**

This story took place when Jesus was traveling all over the country, teaching about God's love and power. Jesus' special friends, or disciples, traveled with him wherever he went. One day, the disciples began to argue about who would be the greatest when they got to heaven. Since they'd been traveling with Jesus for so long, each disciple thought he was more important than the other. Finally they asked Jesus, "Who is the greatest in the kingdom of heaven?"

Jesus called a little child to stand in front of him. Then Jesus said to his disciples, "I tell you the truth, you must change and become like little children. Otherwise, you will never enter the kingdom of heaven. The greatest person in the kingdom of heaven is the one who makes himself humble like this child."

Jesus didn't mean that only children can go to heaven! He wanted his friends to understand that they were being selfish and full of pride. Jesus told them not to be so stuck-up! Instead, he wanted them to be humble and trusting, like little children. Just like it was hard for me to enter the story area, it's hard for proud, selfish people to enter God's kingdom.

Jesus is with us.

Jesus also told his friends that children are very important. He said, "Be careful. Don't think these little children are worth nothing. I tell you that they have angels in heaven who are always with my Father in heaven." You children are so important that God sends angels to watch over each one of you!

Later, some parents brought their children to Jesus. They wanted God's Son to put his hands on the children and pray for them. Ask:

● **What do you think it would be like to have Jesus pray for you?** (Neat because he's God's Son; it would make me feel special!)

Say: **These parents wanted Jesus to bless their children. But Jesus' friends told them to go away. They thought Jesus was too busy to bother with children. But Jesus said, "Let the little children come to me. Don't stop them, because the kingdom of heaven belongs to people who are like these children." Again, Jesus reminded his friends that it's important to be like a child. He wanted them to know that children are special to him because children are loving and full of trust.**

Put the *Bible Big Book* away and out of sight. Ask:

● **What did Jesus say about children?** (That they're important; that other people should trust him like children do; that angels watch over us.)

● **Why did Jesus' friends want to stop the children?** (They thought Jesus didn't care about children; they thought Jesus was too busy.)

● **How does Jesus watch over you?** (He sends angels; he loves me all the time; his angels protect me.)

● **Why is it good to know that Jesus is with you?** (Because I'll never be alone; because I love him; because he takes care of me.)

Say: **Jesus is with us all the time. He loves you so much that he has angels watch over you night and day. No matter where you go or what you do, Jesus is there! Let's play a game to think of all the times and places that Jesus is with us.**

● **The Point**

Do the Bible Story (up to 10 minutes)

Before this activity, use yarn or string to make a circle on the floor and divide it into three sections. The circle should be large enough for everyone to stand around. Photocopy the "All the Time" handout (p. 139) and enlarge the figures if possible. Cut out the figures of a child waking up, sleeping, and swinging and tape them in separate sections of the circle. Have children stand outside the circle.

Say: **This circle is kind of like a clock. Each part of the circle shows a different time of day. The picture of the child stretching is the morning, the picture of the child swinging is the afternoon, and the picture of the child lying in bed is nighttime. When I start the music, start walking around the clock. Keep walking until I stop the music, then stand still where you are. Ready?**

Play "Walk Around the Clock" (track 19) on the *CD* for a few seconds, then pause the *CD*.

Say: **Look at the picture in front of you and think of something you do at that time of day.** Allow children to think for a moment, then call on several children to share. Children may say things like "I eat breakfast in the morning," "I like to play in the afternoon," or "I have to take a bath at night." When several children have shared, lead children in shouting, **"Jesus is the**

rock! He's the rock around the clock!" Then start the music and play again. You may want to have children hop, skip, walk heel-to-toe, or take giant steps as they move around the circle. Be sure each child has a chance to share at least once, then have children sit down around the circle.

● The Point

Say: **Jesus always has time for us—he's our rock! He's strong for us when we're weak and ● he's with us all the time. Everywhere you go and in everything you do... Jesus will be there just for you! You know, Pockets looked awfully sad this morning when I saw her. Let's see if we can cheer her up with what we've learned today.**

Practicing the Point

Missing Mommy (up to 5 minutes)

Bring out Pockets the Kangaroo and go through the following puppet script. When you finish the script, put Pockets away and out of sight.

Missing Mommy

PUPPET SCRIPT

(Pockets bounds out, cheerfully chanting, "Jesus is the rock! He's the rock around the clock!")

Pockets: Hi, everyone! I'm so glad I got to come here today! All of you make me feel better when I come to class.

Teacher: Well, Pockets, that's certainly a nice thing to say. I thought you were feeling sad this morning. What happened?

Pockets: *(Giggles.)* Yeah, I sure was feeling sad. I was lower than a kangaroo's tail! My mom went to take care of my aunt, who just had a baby. I really missed my mom! I wished that she was home to make me breakfast, tie my hair bows, brush my fur, and kiss me good night. Missing her made me sad!

Teacher: I know what it's like to miss someone. But what happened to make you so cheerful?

Pockets: Well, I was sitting here, feeling sad and sorry for myself, when I heard you all playing and shouting about Jesus. You were saying, "Jesus is the rock! He's the rock around the clock!"

Teacher: Yes, we certainly were! We heard a story about Jesus and some children. Who can tell Pockets what Jesus said about the children? *(Call on children to share about today's story and that Jesus is with them all the time.)* That's why we're so excited.

Pockets: See, that's why I love coming to class! I always learn something. Well, when I heard you shouting about Jesus, I started thinking. Knowing that Jesus is with me all the time made me feel better about my mom being gone. In fact, it made me super happy! 'Cause Jesus can go places with me where even my mom can't go... like to kangaroo school, to soccer practice, to Sarah's house... everywhere!

(Continued)

Jesus is with us.

Teacher: Pockets, I'm sure glad you came today! You really understand that Jesus is with us all the time.

Pockets: Yep, and now I'm so cheerful that I'm going to make my new cousin a happy birthday card. 'Bye, everyone.

◐ **The Point**

TODAY I LEARNED...

We believe that Christian education extends beyond the classroom into the home. Photocopy the "Today I Learned..." handout (p. 152) for this week and send it home with your children. Encourage parents to use the handout to plan meaningful family activities to reinforce this week's topic. Follow up the "Today I Learned..." activities next week by asking children what their families did.

Closing

Open Your Eyes! (up to 5 minutes)

Say: **Pockets' happiness rubbed off on me! I feel like singing! Let's sing a song about all the times and places Jesus is with us. It will remind us that Jesus loves us all the time!** Lead children in singing "Jesus Is Always There" (track 20) to the tune of "Ten Little Indians" with the *CD*.

Sing

Jesus loves me in the morning.
Jesus loves me in the noontime.
Jesus loves me in the evening.
He is always there!

Jesus loves me when I'm playing.
Jesus loves me when I'm sleeping.
Jesus loves me when I'm talking.
He is always there!

Jesus loves me in the morning.
Jesus loves me in the noontime.
Jesus loves me in the evening.
He is always there!

Form pairs and say: **Now tell your partner where you'll look for Jesus this week. Maybe it'll be at school, at the playground, at the library, or when you go to bed at night.**

When children have finished sharing, pray: **Dear God, thank you that you send angels to watch over us all the time. And thank you that Jesus is with us, too. Help us remember that he's always there and that we can talk to him whenever we want to. In Jesus' name, amen.**

For Extra Time

If you have a long class time or want to add additional elements to your lesson, try one of the following activities.

LIVELY LEARNING: Tossing Time

Photocopy the "All the Time" handout (p. 139) and cut apart the figures. Form a circle and tape the figures to the floor in the middle of the circle. Give one child the *ring* and say: **Tell us which figure you'll try to toss the *ring* to. Then toss the *ring* and tell us when Jesus will be with you, according to the picture.** Pass the *ring* around so each person has a turn to play.

MAKE TO TAKE: Welcome Bell

Set out jingle bells, a hole punch, scissors, crayons, 6-inch lengths of ribbon, and cardboard or paper tubes. Show children how to punch two holes in the top of their cardboard tubes and two holes in the bottom. Help children tie jingle bells to two lengths of ribbon and tie the ribbons through the holes at the bottom of the tubes. Have each child tie another length of ribbon through the top holes, to make a hanger. Children may decorate the tubes with crayon or bits of wrapping paper. Tell them to hang their welcome bells on doorknobs at home. Remind children that Jesus welcomed the children so he could bless them.

TREAT TO EAT: He's Always Watching!

Give each child half of a bagel or a whole rice cake. Have each child spread flavored cream cheese on the bagel or rice cake, then place 12 chocolate chips or raisins around the outer edge to resemble numbers on a clock. Remind children that no matter what time it is, Jesus is with us.

STORY PICTURE: Jesus Welcomes the Children

Hand each child a photocopy of the "Today I Learned..." handout (p. 152) and have children color the picture. Then distribute the "All the Children" handouts (p. 151). Have children fold and cut out the figures. Help children tape one hand of each child to the picture of Jesus, then tape the other hands together so they make a circle over Jesus. Tell children they can be sure that ● Jesus is with us all the time.

● **The Point**

All the Children

Photocopy and cut out the figures.

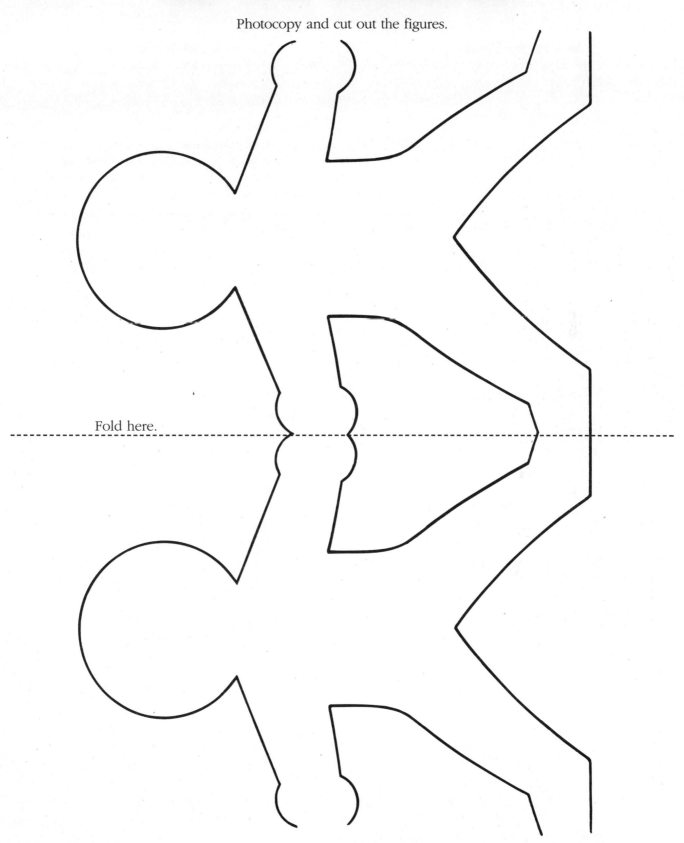

Fold here.

Jesus is with us.

TODAY I LEARNED...

The Point ✏ Jesus is with us all the time.

Today your child learned that Jesus is with us all the time. They discovered that Jesus said children are very important. Children learned that Jesus watches over them, whatever they're doing.

Verse to Learn

"I am with you always, to the very end of the age" (Matthew 28:20b).

Ask Me...

● What did Jesus say about children?
● How do you know that Jesus is with you?
● How does our family show that children are important?

Family Fun

● If you have a clock that chimes or cuckoos, thank Jesus for being with you every time the clock chimes. If you don't have a chiming clock, set a kitchen timer to go off every hour one evening. When you hear the bell, thank Jesus for being with you.

● Make a welcome mat for your home. Get a carpet square (free from most carpet stores) and use acrylic paints or shoe polish to write "Welcome" on it. Let the mat be a reminder that Jesus welcomed little children.

Jesus Welcomes the Children (Matthew 18:1-5, 10; 19:13-15)

Never Alone

The Point

✎ Jesus is with us when we're lonely.

The Bible Basis

John 4:4-30, 39. Jesus talks to a Samaritan woman.

The Samaritan woman who met Jesus at the well is a poignant picture of loneliness and rejection. Not only did her Samaritan heritage make her contemptible to the Jews, but her promiscuity placed her outside the social circles of her own people. To avoid awkward silences and accusing glances, she went to the well in the heat of midday, when no one else would be there. Imagine her surprise when Jesus, a prophet of Jewish heritage, talked openly with her—ignoring social taboos! He named her wrongdoing, then offered her eternal life. With amazement and joy, the woman ran to town and told everyone about the man she'd just met. Jesus had befriended a lonely heart and changed a life—and a town—forever.

Five- and 6-year-olds understand loneliness. When friends move away, families split up, or they have trouble making friends in a new place, children feel abandoned. With Jesus as a forever friend, children can work through their feelings of loneliness and realize that they're never truly alone. Just as Jesus was there for the Samaritan woman, he is here for children today. Use this lesson to help children discover the wonderful truth that Jesus will be with them, even when they're lonely.

Getting the Point

✎ **Jesus is with us when we're lonely.**

It's important to say The Point just as it's written in each activity. Repeating The Point over and over will help the children remember it and apply it to their lives.

Children will
- learn that Jesus never leaves us alone,
- hear how Jesus befriended the lonely Samaritan woman,
- help Pockets realize that Jesus never leaves us, and
- thank Jesus for being with them.

● **The Point**

This Lesson at a Glance

Before the lesson, collect the necessary items for the activities you plan to use. Refer to the Classroom Supplies and Learning Lab Supplies columns to determine what you'll need. Remember to make photocopies of the "Today I Learned . . ." handout (p. 164) to send home with your children.

Section	Minutes	What Children Will Do	Classroom Supplies	Learning Lab Supplies
Welcome Time	up to 5	**Welcome!**—Receive name tags and be greeted by the teacher.	"Star Name Tags" handouts (p. 30), markers, pins or tape	
Let's Get Started Direct children to one or more of the Let's Get Started activities until everyone arrives.	up to 10	**Option 1: See Through Me!**—Make oil pictures to show that Jesus sees their hearts.	Pie tins, cotton balls, clothespins, paper, crayons, baby oil, paper-bag smocks, newspapers	
	up to 10	**Option 2: Well Beings**—Use paper bags and newspapers to build a well.	Paper grocery sacks, newspapers, masking tape, pitcher, water	
	up to 10	**Option 3: Balancing Act**—Balance cups on their heads as they walk along a line.	Paper cups, masking tape, newspaper	
Pick-Up Song	up to 5	**We Will Pick Up**—Sing a song as they pick up toys and gather for Bible-Story Time.	CD player	CD: "We Will Pick Up" (track 2)
Bible-Story Time	up to 5	**Setting the Stage**—Search for friends in silent darkness.		
	up to 5	**Bible Song and Prayer Time**—Sing a song, bring out the Bible, and pray together.	Bible, construction paper, scissors, basket or box, CD player	CD: "God's Book" (track 3), Jesus and Me stamp and ink pad
	up to 10	**Hear the Bible Story**—Hear how Jesus befriended a Samaritan woman in John 4:4-30, 39 and sip cups of water from a "well."	Bible, paper well from Option 2, paper cups, CD player	CD: "Living Water" (track 21), Bible Big Book: Jesus Is With Us
	up to 10	**Do the Bible Story**—Pass along "living water" from the well.	Paper cups, paper well from Option 2	
Practicing the Point	up to 5	**Poor Me!**—Cheer Pockets with the news that Jesus is with her when she feels lonely.	Pockets the Kangaroo, a small stuffed animal	
Closing	up to 5	**Never Alone**—Scatter around the room and sing, then gather to pray.	CD player	CD: "Jesus Is With Me" (#1) (track 22)
For Extra Time		For extra-time ideas and supplies, see page 162.		

Jesus is with us.

Welcome Time

Welcome! (up to 5 minutes)

- Bend down and make eye contact with children as they arrive.
- Greet each child individually with an enthusiastic smile.
- Thank each child for coming to class today.
- As children arrive, ask them about last week's "Today I Learned..." discussion. Ask questions such as "When did you feel Jesus' love?" and "How did you show other children that they're important?"
- Say: **Today we're going to learn that ● Jesus is with us when we're lonely.**

Hand out the star name tags children made in the first lesson and help them attach the name tags to their clothing. If some of the name tags were damaged or if some of the children weren't in class that week, have them make new name tags using the photocopiable patterns on page 30.

- Direct children to the Let's Get Started activities you've set up.

● **The Point**

Let's Get Started

Set up one or more of the following activities for children to do as they arrive. After you greet each child, invite him or her to choose an activity.

Circulate among the children to offer help as needed and direct children's conversation toward today's lesson. Ask questions such as "When do you feel lonely?" or "How can you help others who may be lonely?"

☐ OPTION 1: See Through Me! (up to 10 minutes)

Before class, pour a small amount of baby oil into a pie tin. Help children clip cotton balls to clothespins to make daubers, then cover the table with newspapers. Provide paper-bag smocks for children to wear during this activity.

Set out crayons and give each child two sheets of paper. Instruct them to draw pictures of themselves on one sheet of paper and a heart on the other. Then have children use the daubers to spread baby oil on the pictures of themselves. Lay the oiled drawing on top of the heart drawing and show children that they can see through the top paper! Explain that Jesus sees our hearts and knows when we're lonely.

☐ OPTION 2: Well Beings (up to 10 minutes)

Set out newspapers, masking tape, and paper grocery sacks. Show children how to make large blocks by stuffing the paper sacks with crumpled newspapers, folding the tops down twice, and taping them shut. When children have made a good supply of blocks, allow them to build a round well, as shown in the margin. As they work, tell children that in today's Bible story they'll hear about a lonely woman who got more than water when she went to the well.

When the well is complete, place a clean pitcher of drinking water in the middle.

OPTION 3: Balancing Act (up to 10 minutes)

Before children arrive, make an 8-foot masking tape line on the floor. Show children how to tear newspaper into strips and crumple the strips into little balls. Have each child put three balls in a paper cup, then place the cup on his or her head. Show children how to balance the cups on their heads and walk along the tape line as if it were a tightrope. Explain that in the Bible, women carried pitchers of water on their heads.

When everyone has arrived and you're ready to move on to the Bible-Story Time, encourage the children to finish what they're doing and get ready to clean up.

Pick-Up Song

We Will Pick Up (up to 5 minutes)

Lead children in singing "We Will Pick Up" (track 2) with the *CD* to the tune of "London Bridge." Encourage children to sing along as they help clean up the room.

If you want to include the names of all the children in your class, sing the song without the *CD* and repeat the naming section. If you choose to use the *CD*, vary the names you use each week.

Sing

We will pick up all our toys,
All our toys, all our toys.
We will pick up all our toys
And put them all away.

I see (name) picking up,
Picking up, picking up.
I see (name) picking up
And putting toys away.

(Repeat.)

Bible-Story Time

Setting the Stage (up to 5 minutes)

Tell the children you'll clap your hands to get their attention. Explain that when you clap, the children are to stop what they're doing, raise their hands, and focus on you. Encourage children to respond quickly so you'll have time for all the fun activities you've planned.

Say: **Our class is fun because we're all friends here. But sometimes we go places where we're not surrounded by friends. Let's do an activity to see what that's like. First, spread out so you're not standing near anyone.** Pause for children to follow your instructions. **Now, turn off the volume on your voice box so you can't make any noises. Close your eyes**

Jesus is with us.

and I'll turn off the lights so you can't see, either. When I say "Go," move around slowly, and gently try to join up with everyone in the class to make a giant blob. Remember, no noises and no peeking! Ready? Go!

If your room doesn't get completely dark, use bandannas as blindfolds. When children are all joined together, turn on the lights and have them form a circle and sit down. Then ask:

● **What was it like to try to find your friends?** (Hard; dark; kind of scary; almost impossible.)

● **How did you feel when you found the group?** (Glad; happy; relieved; super.)

Say: **Being lonely is kind of like looking for friends in the dark. It's a bad feeling! But that bad feeling goes away when we realize that** ◗**Jesus is with us when we're lonely. Let's get ready to hear a story about a woman who was very lonely until she met Jesus.**

◗ **The Point**

Bible Song and Prayer Time (up to 5 minutes)

Before class, make surprise cards for this activity by cutting construction paper into 2×6-inch slips. Prepare a surprise card for each child, plus a few extras for visitors. Fold the cards in half, then stamp the *Jesus and Me stamp* inside one of the surprise cards. Mark John 4:4-30, 39 in the Bible you'll be using.

Have children sit in a circle. Say: **Now it's time to choose a Bible person to bring me the Bible marked with today's Bible story. As we sing our Bible song, I'll pass out the surprise cards. Don't look inside your surprise card until the song is over.**

Lead children in singing "God's Book" (track 3) with the *CD* to the tune of "Old MacDonald Had a Farm." As you sing, pass out the folded surprise cards. If you want to include the names of all the children in your class, sing the song without the *CD* and repeat the naming section. If you choose to use the *CD*, vary the names you use each week.

Sing 🎵

Now it's time to read God's Book
And hear a Bible story.
It's fun to be here with my
    friends
And hear a Bible story.

(Name)**'s here.**
(Name)**'s here.**
Here is (name).
Here is (name).
Now it's time to read God's Book
And hear a Bible story.

Now it's time to read God's Book
And hear a Bible story.
It's fun to be here with my
    friends
And hear a Bible story.

(Name)**'s here.**
(Name)**'s here.**
Here is (name).
Here is (name).
Now it's time to read God's Book
And hear a Bible story.

After the song, say: **You may look inside your surprise cards. The person who has the picture of Jesus stamped inside his or her card will be our Bible person for today.**

Jesus is with us.

Identify the Bible person, then have the rest of the children clap for him or her. Ask the Bible person to bring you the Bible. Help the Bible person open the Bible to the marked place and show children where your story comes from. Then have the Bible person sit down.

Say: (Name) **was our special Bible person today. Each week, we'll have only one special Bible person, but each one of you is a special part of our class! Today we're all learning that** **Jesus is with us when we're lonely.**

Let's say a special prayer now and ask Jesus to be with us when we're lonely. I'll pass around this basket. When the basket comes to you, put your surprise card in it and say, "Jesus, be with me when I am lonely."

Pass around the basket or box. When you've collected everyone's surprise card, set the basket aside and pick up the Bible. Lead children in this prayer: **God, thank you for the Bible and all the stories in it. Teach us today that** Jesus is with us when we're lonely. Amen.

Hear the Bible Story (up to 10 minutes)

Bring a stack of paper cups and gather children near the well that was built in Option 2. If you didn't use Option 2, you'll need a pitcher of drinking water and a picture of a well.

Bring out the *Bible Big Book: Jesus Is With Us*. Hold up a Bible and say: **Our Bible story comes from the book of John in the Bible. Our *Bible Big Book* shows us pictures of our Bible story.**

The place where Jesus lived was dry and dusty like a desert. When people got hot and thirsty, they couldn't just turn on a faucet like we can. They had to pull water from a deep well, kind of like this one. Since we're talking about water today, I'll give each of you a cup of water for our story. Please set your cup in front of you until you hear Jesus speaking. Then take a little sip.

Pour water from the pitcher and give each child a cup. Hold up the *Bible Big Book* so children can see pages 2 and 3. Then play "Living Water" (track 21) on the *CD*. When you hear Jesus speak, take a sip from your own cup to help cue children.

When the track is over, turn off the CD player and put the *Bible Big Book* out of sight. Ask:

● **Why was the Samaritan woman lonely?** (Because she didn't have any friends; because no one liked her; she was all alone.)

● **What did Jesus tell her?** (That he could give her living water; that he was the Messiah.)

● **What did the woman do when she found out Jesus was the Messiah?** (Went and told others about Jesus; ran back to town.)

Say: **When Jesus told the woman he could give her living water, he was talking about eternal life. When we accept God's love and forgiveness, he promises us eternal life in heaven. Jesus promises to be with us forever—even when we're lonely.**

● **How can Jesus help you when you're lonely?** (He'll be my friend; his love will be with me; he'll help me feel better.)

Say: **We'll all be lonely sometimes. But when we feel that way, we can remember that** Jesus is with us when we're lonely. **When the Samaritan woman discovered what a wonderful friend Jesus could be, she told everyone else about Jesus' love. Let's finish the water in our**

cups and remember that Jesus is our friend forever.

Do the Bible Story (up to 10 minutes)

Have children take their cups and line up opposite the paper well from Option 2. Say: **When the Samaritan woman told others about Jesus, they believed in him. Let's see what it's like to pass on the good news that Jesus is with us when we're lonely.**

Balance your empty paper cup on your head and walk slowly to the well. Dip your cup in the water and say to the next child in line: **Come and share this living water!** Have that child come, balancing the cup on his or her head. Pour your cup of water into his or her cup. Then have him or her call the next child and so on.

> ✔ Remind children not to drink the water, since it will be passed from cup to cup.

When the last child has poured the water back into your cup, form a circle. Say: **When Jesus told the Samaritan woman about living water, he was talking about being her friend forever.**

● **Why did the woman want to tell others about Jesus?** (Because she knew he was someone special; she was excited about Jesus' love; she wanted others to meet her friend.)

Say: **The Samaritan woman found a special friend in Jesus, then brought the townspeople to meet him. Soon, many of them believed in Jesus, too. We can share God's love with others, too. I wonder if Pockets knows that** **Jesus is with us when we're lonely.**

🔵 **The Point**

Practicing the Point

Poor Me! (up to 5 minutes)

Before this activity, place a small stuffed animal in Pockets' pouch. Bring out Pockets the Kangaroo and go through the following puppet script. When you finish the script, put Pockets away and out of sight.

Poor Me!

PUPPET SCRIPT

Teacher: Pockets, it looks like you've got yourself a special friend.

Pockets: (Sadly) Yeah, this is Sammy. I keep him with me when I'm feeling lonely. That way I don't feel so all alone.

Teacher: Why are you feeling lonely? You have lots of friends here!

Pockets: (Sighing) I know, but I was feeling lonely at kangaroo

(Continued)

school. My friend Sarah didn't want to play with me because another kangaroo brought some really fun toys. *(Sadly)* They played together and left me out.

Teacher: Well, weren't there other kangaroos for you to play with?

Pockets: Yeah, but no one wanted to play in the sandbox with me. They all were playing Hop-a-long Tag. So I played all by myself.

Teacher: *(Hugs Pockets.)* Oh, Pockets, we all feel left out and alone sometimes. But we learned something today that might help cheer you up. Who can tell Pockets about the lonely woman in our story today? *(Call on children to tell Pockets about the Samaritan woman and how Jesus was with her. Have children tell Pockets that Jesus is with them when they're lonely.)*

Pockets: That woman at the well sounded lonely, just like me. And Jesus came and was her friend?

Teacher: He sure was! And he'll be your friend, too! He's even better company than Sammy!

Pockets: Hmmm. I guess it's OK to be alone when Jesus is with me. That way I'm never really alone at all! Did you hear that, Sammy? I'm never alone!

Teacher: The next time you see someone who's lonely, maybe you can tell that person  Jesus is with us when we're lonely.

Pockets: That sounds like a good idea. Thanks for cheering me up, everyone. 'Bye now!

✏ The Point

TODAY I LEARNED...

We believe that Christian education extends beyond the classroom into the home. Photocopy the "Today I Learned..." handout (p. 164) for this week and send it home with your children. Encourage parents to use the handout to plan meaningful family activities to reinforce this week's topic. Follow up the "Today I Learned..." activities next week by asking children what their families did.

Closing

✏ The Point

Never Alone (up to 5 minutes)

Say: **We're going to learn a song that you can sing whenever you feel lonely. And to remind you that  Jesus is with us when we're lonely, scatter all over the room and sit by yourself.**

When children are seated, lead them in singing "Jesus Is With Me" (#1) (track 22) to the tune of "The Farmer in the Dell" along with the *CD*.

Sing

Jesus is with me.
Jesus is with me.
Even when I'm all alone,
Jesus is with me.

(Repeat.)

Say: 🖊 **Jesus is with us when we're lonely.** Have children form a tight circle. Pray: **Dear God, thank you that Jesus is with us when we're lonely. Because he's there, we know we're never alone. Help us to be good friends to others when we see them feeling lonely. In Jesus' name, amen.**

⬤ **The Point**

Jesus is with us.

For Extra Time

If you have a long class time or want to add additional elements to your lesson, try one of the following activities.

LIVELY LEARNING: Balloon Boppin' Fun

Give each child a blown-up balloon, then have children form a large circle and stand facing away from the center. Call out a color and allow children holding balloons of that color to turn around, take two steps in, and bop the balloons in the air and to each other. Then call another balloon color and instruct those children to move in and bop their balloons, too. Continue to call balloon colors until everyone has joined in the balloon boppin' fun. Point out that God's love brings us all together—no one is left out!

MAKE TO TAKE: The Road to Living Water

Before this activity, photocopy the "Road to Living Water" handout (p. 163) and cut apart the pictures. You'll need one for each child.

Set out the handouts, transparent tape, crayons, and clear sandwich bags. Have each child color a picture and place it inside a sandwich bag. Help children seal the bags with transparent tape. Demonstrate how to put a drop of water on the outside of the bag on the picture of the woman at the well. Have children blow the water drop down the curvy road to town.

TREAT TO EAT: Bubblin' Water

Set out assorted fruits, such as mandarin orange slices, maraschino cherries, sliced grape halves, and pineapple chunks. Then pour lemon-lime soda into paper cups. Have children make their own bubbly treats by using toothpicks to drop fruits into their cups of soda. As children enjoy the refreshing snack, explain that Jesus offered the Samaritan woman something much better than water.

STORY PICTURE: The Samaritan Woman

◖ **The Point**

Give each child a photocopy of the "Today I Learned..." handout (p. 164). Have children color the handout with crayons, then color the bricks of the well with wet chalk. Remind children that ◖Jesus is with us when we're lonely.

Jesus is with us.

Road to Living Water

Photocopy the handout and cut apart the pictures.

TODAY I LEARNED...

The Point ✏ Jesus is with us when we're lonely.

Today your child learned that Jesus is with us when we're lonely. Children heard that Jesus comforted the lonely Samaritan woman at the well. They discovered that they're never alone because Jesus is with them.

Verse to Learn

"I am with you always, to the very end of the age" (Matthew 28:20b).

Ask Me...

● Why was the woman at the well lonely?
● When have you felt lonely?
● How can our family reach others who are lonely?

Family Fun

● Make a care package for a lonely neighbor. Include cheerful notes, pictures of your family, and homemade cookies. Deliver your package as a family along with a bright bouquet of flowers.

The Samaritan Woman (John 4:4-30, 39)

Fear Not!

The Point

✏ Jesus is with us when we're afraid.

The Bible Basis

Matthew 8:23-27. Jesus calms the storm.

What began as a simple trip across the Sea of Galilee turned into a terrifying experience for Jesus' disciples. A sudden, violent storm sent huge waves crashing over the small fishing boat. Fearing for their lives, the disciples cried out to Jesus, who was asleep. Jesus stood and commanded the wind and waves to be still. As the wind and waves subsided, the disciples looked at each other in complete amazement. "What kind of man is this?" they asked. "Even the winds and the waves obey him!"

Five- and 6-year-olds know what it is to be afraid. They may be afraid of the dark, of thunder and lightning, of animals, and of neighborhood bullies. Their worst fears may be triggered by a fight between parents or a scary TV show. You can offer children the comfort of knowing that Jesus is with them even in their scariest moments. Use this lesson to help children understand that Jesus can help and comfort us when we're scared, just as he helped the disciples during the storm.

Getting the Point

✏ **Jesus is with us when we're afraid.**

It's important to say The Point just as it's written in each activity. Repeating The Point over and over will help children remember it and apply it to their lives.

Children will
- hear about Jesus calming a storm,
- learn that Jesus is with them when they're afraid,
- teach Pockets that Jesus is watching over her, and
- throw away their fears.

✏ **The Point**

This Lesson at a Glance

Before the lesson, collect the necessary items for the activities you plan to use. Refer to the Classroom Supplies and Learning Lab Supplies columns to determine what you'll need. Remember to make photocopies of the "Today I Learned..." handout (p. 177) to send home with your children.

Section	Minutes	What Children Will Do	Classroom Supplies	Learning Lab Supplies
Welcome Time	up to 5	**Welcome!**—Receive name tags and be greeted by the teacher.	"Star Name Tags" handouts (p. 30), markers, pins or tape	
Let's Get Started Direct children to one or more of the Let's Get Started activities until everyone arrives.	up to 10	**Option 1: Windy Paintings**—Blow paint across strips of poster board.	Blue and green tempera paint, drinking straws, plastic spoons, poster board, scissors, paint shirts, newspapers	
	up to 10	**Option 2: Life-Ring Toss**—Toss a ring over paper wads and pull them in.	Newspapers, yarn or string, masking tape	Ring
	up to 10	**Option 3: Wonderful Waves**—Create a swirly snack to enjoy later.	Graham crackers, frosting, blue food coloring, plastic knives	
Pick-Up Song	up to 5	**We Will Pick Up**—Sing a song as they pick up toys and gather for Bible-Story Time.	CD player	CD: "We Will Pick Up" (track 2)
Bible-Story Time	up to 5	**Setting the Stage**—Listen to fears and be pulled to "safety."	Table, yarn or string	Ring
	up to 5	**Bible Song and Prayer Time**—Sing a song, bring out the Bible, and pray together.	Bible, construction paper, scissors, basket or box, CD player	CD: "God's Book" (track 3), Jesus and Me stamp and ink pad
	up to 10	**Hear the Bible Story**—Act out Matthew 8:23-27 and hear how Jesus calmed a storm.	Bible, table, Windy Paintings from Option 1	*Bible Big Book: Jesus Is With Us*
	up to 10	**Do the Bible Story**—Create a storm and tell what they're afraid of.	CD player	CD: "Jesus Is With Me" (#2) (track 23)
Practicing the Point	up to 5	**Fear Not, Pockets!**—Teach Pockets that Jesus is with her when she's afraid.	Pockets the Kangaroo	
Closing	up to 5	**Goodbye Fear!**—Throw their fears away and pray.	Wastebasket, scrap paper, crayons	
For Extra Time	For extra-time ideas and supplies, see page 176.			

Welcome Time

Welcome! (up to 5 minutes)

- Bend down and make eye contact with children as they arrive.
- Greet each child individually with an enthusiastic smile.
- Thank each child for coming to class today.
- As children arrive, ask them about last week's "Today I Learned..." discussion. Use questions such as "How was Jesus with you this week?" and "How did you help others who were lonely?"
- Say: **Today we're going to learn that ✎ Jesus is with us when we're afraid.**
- Hand out the star name tags children made during Lesson 1 and help them attach the name tags to their clothing. If some of the name tags were damaged or if children weren't in class that week, have them make new name tags using the photocopiable handout on page 30.
- Direct children to the Let's Get Started activities you've set up.

● The Point

Let's Get Started

Set up one or more of the following activities for children to do as they arrive. After you greet each child, invite him or her to choose an activity.

Circulate among children to offer help as needed and direct children's conversation toward today's lesson. Ask questions such as "When are you afraid?" or "How do you think Jesus can help you when you're afraid?"

◻ OPTION 1: Windy Paintings (up to 10 minutes)

Before this activity, cut four 4×36-inch strips of white or blue poster board. Cover an area with newspapers and set out the poster board strips, blue and green tempera paint, drinking straws, and plastic spoons.

Have children put on paint shirts or paper-bag smocks. Show children how to spoon a small amount of blue and green paint on one end of the poster board strips. Then have children use their straws to blow the paint across the poster board. Explain that today's Bible story is about a stormy wind that made giant waves on a lake. Tell children that Jesus' friends were in a boat on the lake and were very afraid! Set the Windy Paintings in a sunny place to dry until "Hear the Bible Story" time.

◻ OPTION 2: Life-Ring Toss (up to 10 minutes)

Have children wad several sheets of newspaper into balls and place them on the floor. Lay a masking tape line on the floor about five feet from the paper wads. Then tie a 10-foot length of string or yarn to the *ring*. Have children take turns tossing the *ring* around the paper wads then pulling them across the tape line. Explain that in today's story, Jesus saved his friends when their boat was in danger during a terrible storm.

✔ Keep the string attached to the ring. You'll use it again in "Setting the Stage."

☐ **OPTION 3: Wonderful Waves (up to 10 minutes)**

Set out graham crackers, plastic knives, and a bowl of frosting. Let children drop a few drops of blue food coloring into the frosting, then take turns stirring until the frosting is tinted blue. Have children spread frosting "waves" on the graham crackers, then place the crackers on a tray or plate. Explain that Jesus and his friends were caught in a storm that had big, scary waves.

✔ For extra fun, provide gummy fish or fish crackers for children to place in the waves!

When everyone has arrived and you're ready to move on to the Bible-Story Time, encourage the children to finish what they're doing and get ready to clean up.

Pick-Up Song

We Will Pick Up (up to 5 minutes)

Lead children in singing "We Will Pick Up" (track 2) with the *CD* to the tune of "London Bridge." Encourage children to sing along as they help clean up the room.

If you want to include the names of all the children in your class, sing the song without the *CD* and repeat the naming section. If you choose to use the *CD,* vary the names you use each week.

Sing

We will pick up all our toys,
All our toys, all our toys.
We will pick up all our toys
And put them all away.

I see (name) picking up,
Picking up, picking up.
I see (name) picking up
And putting toys away.

(Repeat.)

Bible-Story Time

Setting the Stage (up to 5 minutes)

Tell the children you'll clap your hands to get their attention. Explain that when you clap, the children are to stop what they're doing and focus on you. Encourage children to respond quickly so you'll have time for all the fun activities you've planned.

Before this activity, turn a table upside down to make a "boat." If you have more than 10 children in your class, push two overturned tables together to make a large boat.

Stand on the boat and have children sit a few feet away from it. Say: **Let's pretend you're all swimming in a lake and I'm in my nice, safe boat! You must be cold and wet in that lake! Show me how cold you are.** Pause while children shiver and rub their arms to keep warm. **Brrr! I got cold just watching you! I get scared when I'm in cold water. I'd better help you! I know—I'll toss this life preserver to you and pull you into my boat. Here I go. Heave-HO!**

Toss the *ring* (with the string attached) to two or three children and pull them into the boat. Be sure children don't pull on the string, since it won't hold much weight. Then say: **Hmm. Now it's getting dark out on this lake! I'm really afraid of the dark, so I'll pull a few more of you to safety.** Toss the *ring* to a few more children and pull them to the boat. **Yikes! Did you see that lightning? Ooo—listen to the thunder! I get scared during storms! I'd better get some more of you out of the lake before that storm gets any closer!** Toss the *ring* and pull two or three children to the boat. **The rest of you look so lonely out there in the water. Sometimes I get scared when I'm alone. Why don't you come and join the rest of us on the boat?** Pull the rest of the children into the boat. Put the *ring* away and out of sight.

Say: **I feel much better now that we're all safe on our boat. We all get scared sometimes, but today we'll learn that ◗ Jesus is with us when we're afraid. Now let's all get nice and comfortable on our boat and prepare to hear a stormy story!**

◗ **The Point**

Bible Song and Prayer Time (up to 5 minutes)

Before class, make surprise cards for this activity by cutting construction paper into 2×6-inch slips. Prepare a surprise card for each child, plus a few extras for visitors. Fold the cards in half, then stamp the *Jesus and Me stamp* inside one of the surprise cards. Mark Matthew 8:23-27 in the Bible you'll be using.

Have children sit in a circle. Say: **Now it's time to choose a Bible person to bring me the Bible marked with today's Bible story. As we sing our Bible song, I'll pass out surprise cards. Don't look inside your surprise card until the song is over.**

Lead children in singing "God's Book" (track 3) with the *CD* to the tune of "Old MacDonald Had a Farm." As you sing, pass out the folded surprise cards. If you want to include the names of all the children in your class, sing the song without the *CD* and repeat the naming section. If you choose to use the *CD*, vary the names you use each week.

Sing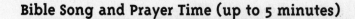

Now it's time to read God's Book
And hear a Bible story.
It's fun to be here with my
    friends
And hear a Bible story.
	Now it's time to read God's Book
	And hear a Bible story.
	It's fun to be here with my
	    friends
	And hear a Bible story.

(Name)'s here. (Name)'s here. Here is (name). Here is (name). Now it's time to read God's Book And hear a Bible story.	(Name)'s here. (Name)'s here. Here is (name). Here is (name). Now it's time to read God's Book And hear a Bible story.

After the song, say: **You may look inside your surprise cards. The person who has the picture of Jesus stamped inside his or her card will be our Bible person for today.**

Identify the Bible person, then have the rest of the children clap for him or her. Ask the Bible person to bring you the Bible. Help the Bible person open the Bible to the marked place and show children where your story comes from. Then have the Bible person sit down.

Say: (Name) **was our special Bible person today. Each week, we'll have only one special Bible person, but each one of you is a special part of our class! Today we're all learning that** 🖊 **Jesus is with us when we're afraid.**

Let's say a special prayer now and ask God to be with us when we're afraid. I'll pass around this basket. When the basket comes to you, put your surprise card in it and say, "God, be with me when I am afraid."

Pass around the basket or box. When you've collected everyone's surprise card, set the basket aside and pick up the Bible. Lead children in this prayer: **God, thank you for the Bible and all the stories in it. Teach us today that** 🖊 **Jesus is with us when we're afraid. Amen.**

🖊 **The Point**

🖊 **The Point**

Hear the Bible Story (up to 10 minutes)

Bring out the *Bible Big Book: Jesus Is With Us*. Have children gather on the boat from "Setting the Stage." Hold up a Bible and say: **Our Bible story comes from the book of Matthew in the Bible. Our *Bible Big Book* shows us pictures of our Bible story. As I tell the story, I'll need a few volunteers to help us act it out.** Choose as many as half the children to stand around the outside of the boat. Show them how to wave the Windy Paintings from Option 1 so the poster board strips make "stormy sounds." Choose one volunteer to be Jesus.

Say: **The children outside the boat are our Storm-makers. They'll make wind, waves, and thunder for our story. The rest of you have an important job, too. You'll be Jesus' disciples. Listen carefully and I'll tell you what to do as the story goes on.**

Read the following story and have children act out the directions in the column on the right.

When Jesus and his disciples visited the city of Capernaum, crowds of people gathered to see and hear him. Many brought sick people for Jesus to heal. All day long people pushed and shoved and crowded together to get close to Jesus. By evening, Jesus was very tired.	*Have Jesus yawn and stretch.*
So he and his friends got into a boat to cross the lake.	*Have the Disciples point across the room.*
While his disciples sailed the boat, Jesus lay down and fell fast asleep.	*Have Jesus lie down and pretend to sleep.*
Suddenly, a dark storm cloud raced across the sky.	*Have the Storm-makers wiggle the Windy Paintings.*
A strong wind whipped the lake into angry waves that splashed over the boat and sent it rocking from side to side.	*Have the Disciples sway back and forth. Hold the Bible Big Book so children can see pages 4 and 5, then lay it aside.*
The boat dipped and crashed in the waves and began to fill up with water. The disciples were terrified! They thought, "If this keeps up, we'll all drown!"	*Have the Disciples act afraid.*
The frightened disciples turned to Jesus who was still fast asleep. They shook him and cried, "Lord, save us! We're going to drown!"	*Have the Disciples shake Jesus.*
Jesus woke up and asked, "Why are you afraid?" Then he got up and spoke to the wind and the waves.	*Have Jesus stand up, face the Storm-makers, and hold out his arms.*

Jesus is with us.

Suddenly, the storm stopped.

The wind died down and the waves became calm. The disciples were amazed! Even the wind and waves obeyed Jesus! His friends weren't afraid anymore.

Have the Storm-makers stop wiggling the Windy Paintings and sit down.

Have the Disciples act surprised.

After you've gone through the story once, have children switch roles and do the story again. Then collect the Windy Paintings and have everyone gather on the boat. Ask:

● **Why were Jesus' friends so scared?** (Because they thought they'd drown; because the storm was scary; because the boat was full of water.)

● **What did Jesus do when they woke him up?** (Made the storm stop; talked to the wind and waves; helped his friends feel better.)

● **What makes you afraid?** (Storms; being alone; big dogs; loud noises; when people fight.)

● **How can Jesus help you feel better?** (He'll be my friend; he'll take those scary things away; he'll protect me.)

Say: **Just as Jesus was there for his frightened friends, ◗ Jesus is with us when we're afraid. Even if it's in the middle of the night, or we're far from home, or at school, Jesus will be there to comfort, love, and protect us. Let's discover more about how Jesus can calm our fears.**

◗ The Point

Do the Bible Story (up to 10 minutes)

Form a circle on the floor. Say: **We're going to create our own rainstorm to remember the storm that Jesus calmed. Follow my instructions and listen to the storm get louder and louder. When the storm is at it's loudest, I'll point to different children. If I point to you, pop up, tell us something that people are afraid of, then sit down. Ready?**

Lead children through the following sequence of motions.

● Rub your fingertips together.

● Rub your palms together.

● Snap your fingers. (Some children may have trouble with this one, but encourage everyone to try.)

● Pat your legs.

● Clap your hands and stomp your feet.

As you point to different children, encourage others to continue the storm noises. When everyone has had a turn to share, lead children in calming the storm by reversing the sequence. Then ask:

● **What do you do when you're afraid?** (Pray; hold my teddy bear; talk to my parents.)

● **Can Jesus make your fears go away? Why?** (Yes, because he's bigger than what I'm afraid of; yes, because he can do anything.)

Say: **We're learning that Jesus is with us all the time—even when we're lonely or afraid. Let's sing the song we learned last week to remind us of Jesus, our forever friend. As we sing, sit shoulder-to-shoulder with your neighbors and move from side to side with the music. That will help us remember that Jesus is with all of us!**

Lead children in singing "Jesus Is With Me" (#2) (track 23) to the tune of "The Farmer in the Dell" along with the *CD*.

Sing

Jesus is with me.
Jesus is with me.
Even when I'm all alone,
Jesus is with me.

Jesus is with me.
Jesus is with me.
Even when I am afraid,
Jesus is with me.

(Repeat.)

Say: 🖊 **Jesus is with us when we're afraid. He wants to comfort and love us through all the storms in our lives. We can comfort our friends, too. Let's share our stormy story with our friend, Pockets.**

● **The Point**

Practicing the Point

Fear Not, Pockets (up to 5 minutes)

Bring out Pockets the Kangaroo and go through the following puppet script. When you finish the script, put Pockets away and out of sight. Have the children sit in a circle.

Fear Not, Pockets!

PUPPET SCRIPT

(Pockets is lying down, snoring softly.)

Teacher: *(Whispers.)* Pockets is asleep! Let's gently wake her up. *(Gently shakes Pockets and whispers.)* Pockets! Pockets!

Pockets: *(Groggy.)* Huh? What? Oh, I must have fallen asleep. *(Yawns.)*

Teacher: Why are you so tired this morning? You're usually bouncing with energy.

Pockets: *(Yawns.)* I didn't sleep very well last night. My night light broke, and I was scared of the dark.

Teacher: Pockets, you know your room is safe.

Pockets: I know, but when it's all dark I imagine that three-headed monsters with long, hairy fingers and bad breath live under my bed. That's scary! I also imagine that bats are hanging from my ceiling, and that . . .

(Continued)

Jesus is with us.

The Point

Teacher: You certainly have an active imagination! It's OK to be afraid. We're all scared sometimes. But today we learned that ⬤ Jesus is with us when we're afraid. He was with his special friends when they were afraid, too. Children, can you tell Pockets what happened to the disciples? *(Have children tell Pockets about Jesus calming the storm.)*

Pockets: Ooooh, I'd be really scared on a stormy lake! There might be crocodiles, snakes, whales, and sea monsters in there!

Teacher: Well, I don't know if Jesus' friends were afraid of those things, but they were definitely afraid. And when they went to Jesus, he calmed the storm and helped their fears go away.

Pockets: Will Jesus do that for me when I'm scared?

Teacher: He certainly will! The next time you're afraid, don't think about monsters—think about Jesus instead! And remember that Jesus promises to be with us when we're afraid.

Pockets: That's good news! *(Yawns.)* I'm so sleepy! Would you mind if I went home to take a nap?

Teacher: Of course not. Sweet dreams, Pockets.

TODAY I LEARNED . . .

We believe that Christian education extends beyond the classroom into the home. Photocopy the "Today I Learned . . ." handout (p. 177) for this week and send it home with your children. Encourage parents to use the handout to plan meaningful family activities to reinforce this week's topic. Follow up the "Today I Learned . . ." activities next week by asking children what their families did.

Closing

Goodbye Fears! (up to 5 minutes)

Form a circle and say: **Pockets might sleep better tonight, knowing that Jesus is with her—even in the dark. Jesus will help take away your fears, too. I'm going to pass out some paper and give you one minute to draw a picture of something that scares you.** Distribute crayons and sheets of office paper (used on one side). After one minute, have children each tell a partner what they drew.

Then say: **We'll all be scared sometimes. But now we know that ⬤ Jesus is with us when we're afraid. You can call on Jesus, just as his disciples did, and Jesus will help your fears go away. Let's get rid of these scary things right now.**

The Point

Place a wastebasket in the middle of the circle. **We'll take turns tossing our papers in the wastebasket and saying, "Jesus is with me when I'm afraid." I'll go first.** When children have tossed all their "fears," lead them in

Jesus is with us.

a prayer similar to this one: **Dear God, thank you for watching over us and loving us all the time. Thank you for Jesus who knows our fears and is with us when we're afraid. Help us call on him whenever we're scared. In Jesus' name, amen.**

If children made the Wonderful Waves snack from Option 3, let them enjoy the snack now.

For Extra Time

If you have a long class time or want to add additional elements to your lesson, try one of the following activities.

LIVELY LEARNING: Boat Races

Take children to an area with a slippery tile floor. Form two groups and have each group make a boat at one end of the room. Have children sit on the floor in a line with their legs outstretched and their hands on the shoulders of the person in front of them. On your signal, have the boats race by scooting to the other side of the room. Be sure children work together to help their boat get to "shore." Remind children that Jesus' friends were scared in their boat, but Jesus calmed their fears.

MAKE TO TAKE: Frothy-Wave Pictures

Have children roll up their sleeves, put on paint shirts or paper-bag smocks, and gather around a table. Place a fist-sized dollop of shaving cream on the table in front of each child. Add two drops of blue food coloring to the shaving cream and instruct children to mix the foam with their hands. Encourage children to fingerpaint pictures of the stormy lake that Jesus and his friends were on. When children have finished their pictures, demonstrate how to place a sheet of heavy paper on top of the design and gently rub over it. Then lift the paper to show the transferred picture.

TREAT TO EAT: Chip Ships

Have children work together to spread a layer of tortilla chip "ships" on a microwavable plate. Allow children to "storm" the ships with grated cheddar cheese. Microwave the ships for a few seconds, or until the cheese melts, then allow children to dip their ships in an "sea" of mild salsa. If you don't have access to a microwave, children will still enjoy the unmelted cheese.

✔ Before preparing the snacks, check to make sure children are not allergic to the ingredients.

STORY PICTURE: Jesus Calms the Storm

● The Point

Give each child a "Today I Learned..." handout (p. 177). Have children color the picture with crayons, then paint the lake with watercolor paints. As they work, remind children that ● **Jesus is with us when we're afraid.**

TODAY I LEARNED...

The Point ✏ Jesus is with us when we're afraid.

Today your child learned that Jesus is with us when we're afraid. Children heard about Jesus calming a storm when his disciples were afraid. They discovered that they can call on Jesus to help them, too.

Verse to Learn

"I am with you always, to the very end of the age" (Matthew 28:20b).

Ask Me...

● Why were Jesus' friends afraid?
● When are you afraid?
● How can our family remember that Jesus is with us when we're afraid?

Family Fun

● Have family members make a Fear-Fighters Feast to remember that Jesus calmed the storm. Hollow out half a loaf of French bread and have family members tell about things that make them afraid. Then fill the bread shells with tuna salad and share how Jesus helps us when we're afraid. As you enjoy your tuna "boat" sandwiches, remember that Jesus calmed his disciples' fears when he stilled the storm.

Jesus Calms the Storm (Matthew 8:23-27)

LESSON 13

Sad Face, Glad Face

The Bible Basis

Luke 8:40-42, 49-56. Jesus heals Jairus' daughter.

When Jesus returned to Galilee, a crowd of anxious people welcomed him. Jairus, a synagogue leader and prominent member of the community, pushed through the throng, fell at Jesus' feet, and begged Jesus to heal his dying daughter. As Jesus and Jairus made their way to Jairus' house, a messenger brought news that the girl had already died. The messenger added hopelessly, "Don't bother the teacher any more." But Jesus comforted Jairus and told him, "Believe, and she will be healed." As Jesus held the girl's hand, life returned to her body and she immediately stood up. Jesus turned a house of mourning into a house of joy!

Although 5- and 6-year-olds are usually bouncy, happy, little people, their tender spirits are fragile and they easily dissolve in tears. Although they don't handle grief in the same way adults do, children feel it keenly when a friend moves away, a pet dies, or someone they love is sick. We can help children by teaching them that they don't need to face sadness alone because Jesus understands and will comfort them. Use this lesson to help children realize that Jesus is right beside them when they're sad.

Getting the Point

🖉 **Jesus is with us when we're sad.**

It's important to say The Point just as it's written in each activity. Repeating The Point over and over will help the children remember it and apply it to their lives.

Children will
● learn that Jesus cares when they're sad,
● discover that Jesus can heal their hurts, and
● think of ways they can cheer up sad friends.

● **The Point**

This Lesson at a Glance

Before the lesson, collect the necessary items for the activities you plan to use. Refer to the Classroom Supplies and Learning Lab Supplies columns to determine what you'll need. Remember to make photocopies of the "Today I Learned..." handout (p. 190) to send home with your children.

Section	Minutes	What Children Will Do	Classroom Supplies	Learning Lab Supplies
Welcome Time	up to 5	**Welcome!**—Receive name tags and be greeted by the teacher.	"Star Name Tags" handouts (p. 30), markers, pins or tape	
Let's Get Started Direct children to one or more of the Let's Get Started activities until everyone arrives.	up to 10	**Option 1: From Sobs to Smiles**—Record themselves laughing and crying.	Cassette recorder, cassette tape	
	up to 10	**Option 2: Sad Snacks**—Make sad-faced cookies.	Plain sugar cookies, frosting, raisins, licorice whips, plastic knives	
	up to 10	**Option 3: Blue Balloons**—Make faces on balloons.	Balloons, markers, paper grocery sacks	
Pick-Up Song	up to 5	**We Will Pick Up**—Sing a song as they pick up toys and gather for Bible-Story Time.	CD player	CD: "We Will Pick Up" (track 2)
Bible-Story Time	up to 5	**Setting the Stage**—Try to make each other laugh.		
	up to 5	**Bible Song and Prayer Time**—Sing a song, bring out the Bible, and pray together.	Bible, construction paper, scissors, basket or box, CD player	CD: "God's Book" (track 3), Jesus and Me stamp and ink pad
	up to 10	**Hear the Bible Story**—Hold up their balloons as they listen to Matthew 8:40-42, 49-56 and hear how Jesus brought joy to a sad family.	Bible, Blue Balloons from Option 3, CD player, Sad Snacks from Option 2	*Bible Big Book: Jesus Is With Us,* CD: "Jairus' Joy" (track 24)
	up to 10	**Do the Bible Story**—Follow instructions to cheer up a sad partner.	CD player	CD: "Jesus Is With Me" (#3) (track 25)
Practicing the Point	up to 5	**The Crying Kangaroo**—Cheer up Pockets when she can't go on a special trip.	Pockets the Kangaroo, handkerchief or tissue	
Closing	up to 5	**On a Roll**—Wrap around each other in a special hug and pray.		
For Extra Time		For extra-time ideas and supplies, see page 188.		

Jesus is with us.

Welcome Time

Welcome! (up to 5 minutes)

- Bend down and make eye contact with children as they arrive.
- Greet each child individually with an enthusiastic smile.
- Thank each child for coming to class today.
- As children arrive, ask them about last week's "Today I Learned..." discussion. Use questions such as "When were you afraid?" and "How did God help you when you were afraid?"
- Say: **Today we're going to learn that  Jesus is with us when we're sad.**
- Hand out the star name tags children made during Lesson 1 and help them attach the name tags to their clothing. If some of the name tags were damaged or if children weren't in class that week, have them make new name tags using the photocopiable handout on page 30.
- Direct children to the Let's Get Started activities you've set up.

◉ The Point

Let's Get Started

Set up one or more of the following activities for children to do as they arrive. After you greet each child, invite him or her to choose an activity.

Circulate among children to offer help as needed and direct children's conversation toward today's lesson. Ask questions such as "What makes you sad?" or "How does your family help you when you're sad?"

OPTION 1: From Sobs to Smiles (up to 10 minutes)

Set out a cassette recorder loaded with a blank cassette tape. Invite children to record themselves laughing their happiest laugh and crying their saddest cry. Allow children to play back the cassette and identify one another's laughing and crying. Explain that today they'll hear about a man who was very sad until Jesus made him happy.

OPTION 2: Sad Snacks (up to 10 minutes)

Set out plain sugar cookies, bowls of white frosting, raisins, plastic knives, and 4-inch lengths of thin red licorice whips. Let children spread frosting on the cookies then add raisin eyes and noses. Demonstrate how to bend the licorice whips into frowns and place them on the cookies. Have children set the cookies on a plate or tray. Tell children that today they'll learn that ◉ Jesus is with us when we're sad.

OPTION 3: Blue Balloons (up to 10 minutes)

Before class, blow up one balloon per child plus a few extras in case some balloons pop. Set out the balloons and markers and have each child draw a sad face on his or her balloon. Encourage children to be creative and gentle so they don't pop the balloons. As children work, tell them that today's Bible

◉ The Point

● The Point

story is about a family who learned that ● Jesus is with us when we're sad. Store the balloons in paper grocery sacks until "Hear the Bible Story."

When everyone has arrived and you're ready to move on to the Bible-Story Time, encourage the children to finish what they're doing and get ready to clean up.

Pick-Up Song

We Will Pick Up (up to 5 minutes)

Lead children in singing "We Will Pick Up" (track 2) with the *CD* to the tune of "London Bridge." Encourage children to sing along as they help clean up the room.

If you want to include the names of all the children in your class, sing the song without the *CD* and repeat the naming section. If you choose to use the *CD,* vary the names you use each week.

Sing

We will pick up all our toys,
All our toys, all our toys.
We will pick up all our toys
And put them all away.

I see (name) **picking up,**
Picking up, picking up.
I see (name) **picking up**
And putting toys away.

(Repeat.)

Bible-Story Time

Setting the Stage (up to 5 minutes)

Tell the children you'll clap your hands to get their attention. Explain that when you clap, the children are to stop what they're doing, raise their hands, and focus on you. Encourage children to respond quickly so you'll have time for all the fun activities you've planned.

Form a circle on the floor and say: **You'll each have a chance to make somcone smile in this fun game! I'll choose someone to be a Clown. The Clown may walk to anyone in the circle and say, "Be my Clown. Please don't frown" in a serious, silly, or strange way. If that person can say, "I can't be a Clown. Look at my frown" without laughing or smiling, the Clown must try again on someone else. If the person laughs or smiles, he or she becomes the next Clown. So put on your sad faces and try your hardest not to giggle!**

Play until all the children have had a turn, then say: **Now I want to see everyone smile! That's much better!** Ask:

● **What kinds of things make you sad in real life?** (When someone gets sick; when I can't do something I want to do really bad; seeing other people who are sad.)

● **When you're sad, what cheers you up?** (If something good happens; talking to my mom or dad; playing outside; hugging my dog.)

Say: **We'll all be sad sometimes. But when we feel that way, we can remember that**  **Jesus is with us when we're sad. Today we'll hear a story about a family who sure had a reason to be sad. But when they trusted Jesus, he took their sadness away.**

● **The Point**

Bible Song and Prayer Time (up to 5 minutes)

Before class, make surprise cards for this activity by cutting construction paper into 2×6-inch slips. Prepare a surprise card for each child, plus a few extras for visitors. Fold the cards in half, then stamp the *Jesus and Me stamp* inside one of the surprise cards. Mark Luke 8:40-42, 49-56 in the Bible you'll be using.

Have children sit in a circle. Say: **Now it's time to choose a Bible person to bring me the Bible marked with today's Bible story. As we sing our Bible song, I'll pass out surprise cards. Don't look inside your surprise card until the song is over.**

Lead children in singing "God's Book" (track 3) with the *CD* to the tune of "Old MacDonald Had a Farm." As you sing, pass out the folded surprise cards. If you want to include the names of all the children in your class, sing the song without the *CD* and repeat the naming section. If you choose to use the *CD*, vary the names you use each week.

Sing

Now it's time to read God's Book
And hear a Bible story.
It's fun to be here with my
    friends
And hear a Bible story.

(Name)'s here.
(Name)'s here.
Here is (name).
Here is (name).
Now it's time to read God's Book
And hear a Bible story.

Now it's time to read God's Book
And hear a Bible story.
It's fun to be here with my
    friends
And hear a Bible story.

(Name)'s here.
(Name)'s here.
Here is (name).
Here is (name).
Now it's time to read God's Book
And hear a Bible story.

After the song, say: **You may look inside your surprise cards. The person who has the picture of Jesus stamped inside his or her card will be our Bible person for today.**

Identify the Bible person, then have the rest of the children clap for him or her. Ask the Bible person to bring you the Bible. Help the Bible person open the Bible to the marked place and show children where your story comes from. Then have the Bible person sit down.

Say: (Name) **was our special Bible person today. Each week, we'll have only one special Bible person, but each one of you is a special part of our class! Today we're all learning that**  **Jesus is with us when we're sad.**

● **The Point**

Let's say a special prayer now and ask Jesus to be with us when we're sad. I'll pass around this basket. When the basket comes to you, put your surprise card in it and say, "Jesus, please be with me when I am sad."

Pass around the basket or box. When you've collected everyone's surprise card, set the basket aside and pick up the Bible. Lead children in this prayer: **God, thank you for the Bible and all the stories in it. Teach us today that**  **Jesus is with us when we're sad. Amen.**

● **The Point**

Hear the Bible Story (up to 10 minutes)

Bring out the *Bible Big Book: Jesus Is With Us.* Have children gather around you. Hold up the Bible and say: **Our Bible story comes from the book of Luke in the Bible. Our *Bible Big Book* shows us pictures of our Bible story. Let's look back at the stories we've heard over the past three weeks.**

Open the *Bible Big Book* to page 1. Say: **The story of Jesus and the children reminds me that Jesus is only with us sometimes.**
● **Is that right?** (No.)
● **What *did* we hear in this story?** (Jesus is with us all the time; Jesus never leaves us; God sends angels to watch over us.)

Say: **Oh, that's right! Jesus is with us all the time!** Turn to pages 2-3. **This story of the Samaritan woman at the well was a great one! It reminds me that Jesus is only with us if we have lots and lots of friends.**
● **Is that right?** (No.)
● **Who can tell me what you remember about this story?** (Jesus was with the woman when she was lonely; Jesus is with us when we're alone; the woman didn't have any friends.) **Now I remember! I'm so glad you have such good memories!**

Turn to pages 4-5. Say: **Wow! Look at this storm! I'd sure be afraid if I were in that boat.**
● **Didn't we learn that Jesus is with us only if we're brave?** (No.)
● **Am I wrong again?** (Yes!)
● **Who can tell me what we learned last week?** (Jesus is with us when we're afraid; Jesus was with his friends in the boat; Jesus calmed the storm.)

Say: **Oh, of course! We've heard about Jesus being with lots of people in the Bible. Today we'll learn how Jesus was with a family at a very sad time. As you listen to the story, hold up your sad-faced balloon when you hear the words "daughter" or "little girl."**

Distribute the sad-faced balloons from Option 3. Then open the *Bible Big Book* to pages 6 and 7 and play "Jairus' Joy" (track 24) on the *CD.* Turn to page 8 at the sound of the chime.

Close the *Bible Big Book* and ask:
● **Why was Jairus so sad?** (Because his daughter was dying; he thought his daughter was dead.)
● **How did Jesus help Jairus?** (He healed Jairus' daughter; he brought her back to life; he told Jairus not to be afraid.)
● **How does Jesus help you when you're sad?** (He makes things better; he gives me someone to talk to; I remember that he can do anything.)

● **The Point**

Say: **Just as Jesus was with Jairus and his family,** ● **Jesus is with us when we're sad. He'll comfort and love us and help take away the sad feelings! Let's get rid of those sad feelings right now. On the count of three, sit on your balloon and pop that sad face! Ready? One, two, three!**

When all the balloons are popped, say: **Now I feel so happy...and hungry! Let's enjoy something to eat, just like Jairus' daughter did!**

Distribute the Sad Snacks and have children turn their licorice frowns into smiles before eating them. After everyone has finished, move on to the next activity.

Do the Bible Story (up to 10 minutes)

Say: **Even though  Jesus is with us when we're sad, good friends can help each other through sad times, too. In this game, you'll help a sad friend feel glad!**

Form two teams and have them line up at opposite ends of the room, so each person is facing a partner from the other team. You may want to arrange the teams so children have partners of the same sex. Designate one group as Team A and the other as Team B. Read the following list and have children follow your instructions.

- **Team A: Your partner's dog hurt its paw. Skip across the room, give your partner a hug, then skip back.**
- **Team B: Your partner is too sick to go on a class field trip. Twirl across the room, bow to your partner, and tell him or her to feel better, then twirl back.**
- **Team A: Your partner just found a flat tire on his or her bike. Hop across the room, twirl your partner in a circle, then dance back.**
- **Team B: Your partner's best friend just moved far away. Hopscotch across the room, give your partner a quick shoulder rub, then hopscotch back.**
- **Everyone is sad because a storm came and we had to cancel a picnic. Walk backward until you gently bump into a new partner, and tell your partner that things will be OK.**

Have partners sit down together. Ask:
- **What was it like to cheer someone up?** (Fun; nice; great; it made me feel good, too.)
- **What other things can you do to help people who are sad?** (Just love them; let them know I care; give them a hug; pray for them.)

Say: **One way to cheer people up is to remind them that  Jesus is with us when we're sad. Let's remember that by singing "Jesus Is With Me." First, join another pair to form a group of four. Hold hands high over your heads and wave your arms back and forth as you sing.**

Lead children in singing "Jesus Is With Me" (#3) (track 25) to the tune of "The Farmer in the Dell" with the *CD*.

Sing

Jesus is with me.
Jesus is with me.
Even when I'm all alone,
Jesus is with me.

Jesus is with me.
Jesus is with me.
Even when I am afraid,
Jesus is with me.

Jesus is with me.
Jesus is with me.
Even when I'm feeling sad,
Jesus is with me.

⚫ The Point

⚫ The Point

Jesus is with us.

● **The Point**   Say: **Just as Jesus was with Jairus and his family,** ● **Jesus is with us when we're sad. Let's leave sadness behind and visit our cheery friend, Pockets!**

Practicing the Point

The Crying Kangaroo (up to 5 minutes)

Before this activity, tape a facial tissue or handkerchief to Pockets' paw. Have children sit in a circle. Take out Pockets the Kangaroo puppet and go thought the following script.

The Crying Kangaroo
PUPPET SCRIPT
(Pockets is sniffing and dabbing her eyes with a facial tissue.)

Teacher: What's the matter, Pockets?

Pockets: Oh, I'm so sad! Boohoo!

Teacher: *(Hugs Pockets.)* Why are you so sad?

Pockets: My family was going on a special trip to see my grandma. It was going to be so fun, too. On our way, we were going to stop at a zoo, and an ice-cream shop, and an amusement park. But now... *(starts to cry again)* now we can't go!

Teacher: That sounds like a fun trip. Why can't you go?

Pockets: I have a sore throat, and the doctor said I can't go on a long trip like that. He said I need to rest, drink lots of juice, and finish my medicine before I can go. I'm just so sad that we can't go on our fun trip.

Teacher: We're all sad sometimes, Pockets. Today we heard about a man who was very, very sad! Children, let's tell Pockets what happened to Jairus. *(Allow children to explain that Jairus' daughter was dying but Jesus healed her.)*

Pockets: So Jesus turned Jairus' sadness to gladness! That's great...but I wish he could do that for me.

Teacher: Pockets, Jesus is with you when you're sad. He knows how you feel and loves you very much. Jesus won't always make the sad feelings go away right away, but he'll be your friend and make things turn out for the best.

Pockets: And Jesus gave me all of my special friends here to cheer me up. I guess I do feel a little better.

Teacher: Why don't you join us for our Closing time? I'm sure being with your friends will help those sad feelings go away.

Pockets: OK! Let's go!

Jesus is with us.

TODAY I LEARNED ...

We believe that Christian education extends beyond the classroom into the home. Photocopy the "Today I Learned..." handout (p. 190) for this week and send it home with your children. Encourage parents to use the handout to plan meaningful family activities to reinforce this week's topic. Follow up the "Today I Learned..." activities next week by asking children what their families did.

Closing

On a Roll (up to 5 minutes)

Say: **When you're sad, sometimes the best thing anyone can give you is a simple hug. Since Pockets is feeling sad today, let's close with a cinnamon-roll hug and a prayer.** Have children hold hands and stand in a line. (Be sure to include Pockets!) Show the first person in line how to turn to the right, and continue turning around until everyone is rolled into a "cinnamon roll."

Say: **Let's hug our friends as we pray.** Pray: **Dear God, thank you for being with us today as we learned about you. We're glad that ✎ Jesus is with us when we're sad. Teach us to be your helpers when others are sad. In Jesus' name, amen.**

● **The Point**

For Extra Time

If you have a long class time or want to add additional elements to your lesson, try one of the following activities.

LIVELY LEARNING: *Bible Big Book* Listening Center

For a fun review of this module's Bible stories, invite children to listen to the entire *Bible Big Book: Jesus Is With Us* with the *CD*. Choose two children to hold the Big Book and turn the pages at the chimes. The entire story is track 26 on the *CD*.

MAKE TO TAKE: Smiles to Go!

Make enough photocopies of the "Smiles to Go!" handout (p. 189) for each child to have one. Demonstrate how to fold the handout in half the long way, cut along the dotted "smile" lines, then unfold the paper. Help children fold the paper in half along the solid line, then in half again to form a card. As they make the last fold, show children how to pull the smile forward so it pops up when the card is opened. Allow children to decorate the cards with crayons or markers. Tell children to give their cards away to cheer up someone who is sad.

TREAT TO EAT: Beaming Bananas

Slice several bananas in half the long way and give each child a banana "smile." Set out frosting and mini-marshmallows and have children decorate their bananas with marshmallow "teeth." Encourage children to tell about times when their feelings changed from sad to glad.

STORY PICTURE: Jesus Heals Jairus' Daughter

Give each child a copy of the "Today I Learned..." handout on page 190. Have children color the handout, then glue fabric scraps to the bed where Jairus' daughter is lying. As children work, remind them that Jesus was with Jairus when Jairus was sad.

Smiles to Go!

Photocopy this handout. Fold it in half the long way, then cut along the dotted lines. Open it, fold it in half on the solid line, then fold in half again to make a pop-up card.

Jesus is with us.

TODAY I LEARNED...

The Point Jesus is with us when we're sad.

LESSON 13

Today your child learned that Jesus is with us when we're sad. Children heard that Jesus healed Jairus' daughter and made Jairus very happy. They thought of ways they could cheer up sad people, too.

Verse to Learn

"I am with you always, to the very end of the age" (Matthew 28:20b).

Ask Me...

● What did Jairus want Jesus to do?
● How does Jesus comfort you when you're sad?
● Why does God want our family to help people who are sad?

Family Fun

● Fill a jar with brightly colored candies and set it on the dining room table. When family members are sad, invite them to take two "Happy Candies" along with a hug.
● When your family is feeling down, cheer everyone up with a Frown Contest. Have everyone make silly, frowning faces and see who can hold theirs the longest without laughing.

Jesus Heals Jairus' Daughter (Luke 8:40-42, 49-56)

Tell us what you think

Please help Group Publishing continue to provide innovative and exciting resources to help your children know, love, and follow Christ. Please take a moment to fill out and fax or mail back this survey. Thank you!

1. What level(s) and what quarter(s) of Hands-On Bible Curriculum™ are you using?

2. How many children are in your class? adult helpers?

3. How has the size of your class changed since using Hands-On Bible Curriculum?
   - ❑ Remained the same
   - ❑ Grown a little
   - ❑ Grown a lot
   - ❑ Other _____

   Comments:

4. When do you use Hands-On Bible Curriculum?
   - ❑ Sunday school
   - ❑ Children's church
   - ❑ Midweek group
   - ❑ Other (please describe) _____
   _____

5. What do you like best about the curriculum?

6. Is there anything about the curriculum you would like to see changed? (For example, if a certain lesson didn't work well, what specific changes would you recommend?)

7. What products would you like to see Group Publishing develop to fill specific needs in your church?

Name_____   Church Name _____

Denomination _____   Church Size _____

Church Address _____

City _____   State _____   ZIP _____

Church Phone _____   E-mail _____

Fax to: 970-292-4360 or mail to: Group Publishing, Inc., ATTN: Marketing, P.O. Box 485, Loveland, CO 80539.

Check out these Great Resources for Your Children's Ministry!

 Bible Big Books Supplement Any Lesson

Teachers love holding the attention of little ones with these exciting oversized story books. The following titles are included in Winter 2003 curriculum and can be ordered separately:

Zacchaeus (Preschool)   ISBN 1-55945-575-6
Jesus Is With Us (Pre-K & K)   ISBN 1-55945-580-2

Also available – great for the Christmas season: **Jesus' Birth** (1-55945-428-8)

We have 21 additional titles of Bible Big Books available for purchase! Supplement any children's program with these great resources. For a complete list of Bible Big Books, visit our website at **www.HandsOnBible.com**.

 Plush Puppets – the Perfect Teaching Assistant

Kids love learning the Bible with these cute and cuddly puppets.

Cuddles the Lamb Puppet   Item 646847-10444-2
Whiskers the Mouse Puppet   Item 8467
Pockets the Kangaroo Puppet   Item 646847-10442-8

 NEW! Playful Songs and Bible Stories for Preschoolers

Songs, finger plays, hand motions, and interactive story readings combine with 75 important Bible stories. Teachers will find the two audio CDs helpful—both include words and music. Scripture and topic indexes make lesson planning easy! (Sheet music not included.)

ISBN 0-7644-2534-X